THE AUGSBURG CONFESSION:

A Contemporary Commentary

by George W. Forell

Augsburg Publishing House
Minneapolis, Minnesota

THE AUGSBURG CONFESSION

Copyright © 1968 George W. Forell

Library of Congress Catalog Card No. 68-25798

This volume is a revision of articles that appeared originally in *The Lutheran* Vol. 5, Nos. 1-26, published in 1967.

Scripture quotations are from the Revised Standard Version of the Bible, copyright 1946 and 1952 by the Division of Christian Education of the National Council of Churches.

Quotations from the Augsburg Confession are taken from *The Book of Concord,* translated and edited by Theodore G. Tappert, copyright © 1959 Fortress Press, Philadelphia, Pa.

Manufactured in the United States of America

In Memory of

Frederick Joachim Forell
1888 - 1968

My Father Who Taught Me

to Love the Augsburg Confession

The full text of the Augsburg Confession as quoted in this book is available in booklet form as well as being printed together with the other symbols of the Lutheran Church in the Book of Concord.

Introduction

Politics is big business. Cities compete with each other to become the seat of government because of the economic benefits they hope to secure. Centers of political power attract money. This is as true in America as it is in Europe. Many states in the Union have wild tales to tell about the manner in which their state capital was chosen. Often they are stories full of blackmail, bribery, and corruption.

It was in an effort to distribute the economic benefits and burdens that the imperial diet, the highest political body of the German empire in the 16th century, met in different German cities at different times. Compared to the American situation, a diet was more like an extended national presidential convention than a session of Congress. The color and confusion at these occasions would remind us of our leap-year revels when we choose a presidential candidate in an atmosphere combining citizenship and circus, commitment and corruption.

The cause of the Reformation had been a regular item of business at such diets a number of times before Augsburg. Luther had appeared at Worms in 1521. There had been diets at Nürnberg in 1522 and 1524, and at Speyer in 1526 and 1529, dealing among other things with the Reformation. In 1530 it was Augsburg's turn. But this time the emperor, the key figure at such a diet, was to be present. Still a young man, just turned 30, Charles V was now ready, after his military and political victories over the king of France and the Roman pope in the 1520's, to turn his attention again to Germany. Two major items of business were on the agenda: the war against the Turks and the Reformation. It was the threat from the Turks, who had surrounded Vienna in 1529, which made it necessary for Charles V to solicit the help of the Protestant princes and cities for the defense of the empire. Thus the invitation to the Diet of Augsburg was couched in rather friendly terms, promising that all sides to the controversy would be heard.

This meant that the Protestants had to prepare and present a statement of their beliefs to the Emperor. The Augsburg Confession is this document. It is a summary of the faith of the advocates of the Reformation and the followers of Martin Luther presented at the Diet of Augsburg on June 25, 1530. Written by Luther's colleague and friend, the layman Philip Melanchthon, it states first positively in 21 articles what the Protestants believe, and later lists some of the alleged abuses in the practice of the church of the time which the signers felt needed correction. The Augsburg Confession was written and presented because of the need of a particular moment in history. We must not forget that the moment which called forth these words was more than 400 years ago. It was confessed in the face of a powerful German emperor and a serious threat from Moslem armies. It was an actual confession of people at a particular time and under specific circumstances. As such, this confession could and should be studied as an important historical document. But it is also the living heritage of the church of the Augsburg Confession, the people we call "Lutherans," whose faith and life have been influenced by this document. We could also study the Augsburg Confession for its significance for the people called "Lutherans."

The Constitution of the United States is a historical document and can and should be studied as such. It is also a living force affecting the daily life of people in the second half of the 20th century. Similarly, the Augsburg Confession could be examined for its possible effect upon the faith and life of the people who gather in the church of the Augsburg Confession. In the articles which are to follow we shall try to discover the vital meaning of the Augsburg Confession for our time. Leaving it to the historians of Christian thought to establish the document's historical setting and importance, we shall try to see if this confession has anything to say to us in our time, and if it may even be able to help us confess our faith more clearly.

There are no more German emperors, and if there are Turks in Vienna, they are tourists or workers who have come to find jobs and hope to be able to send money back to their families in Turkey. The political and economic problems of the world have changed radically. But if human beings have remained essentially the same, as some of us think, then this document, concerned as it is with the nature and destiny of man, is still of value. In our investigation we shall concentrate on this contemporary aspect of the Augsburg Confession. What is its analysis of the human situation and to what extent is this analysis meaningful in our situation today?

One thing, however, we must not forget. This document was not produced in the quiet study of some philosopher or theologian. It was forged in the heat of a great spiritual battle. Signing it was a risk. The men who placed their names under this document jeopardized their position, their property, and even their lives. They may have done so for a variety of motives, but it was a risky business nevertheless. In the 16th century, as today, if you wanted to be safe you didn't sign anything, you didn't get involved, you said, "Go away, we don't want any." The signers of the Augsburg Confession put their money where their mouth was. Some of them lived to regret it; signing this document wasn't just an exercise in calligraphy.

We will not understand the Augsburg Confession unless we get down to the issues it raises which affect our very lives today. Our conviction that such issues abound in this document is the reason for the chapters which follow.

Contents

Article I. God

What would you answer if somebody asked you, "Who are you?" Probably you would give your name and say, "I am John Smith." But if your questioner was not satisfied with this answer and pursued his inquiry further and you would really like to give him some helpful information, you would probably tell him your history. You would say, "I was born in 1930 in New York City, my father was a salesman whose name was Peter Smith, my mother's name was Mary, and I had two brothers and one sister, etc." To explain exactly who you are you would give as detailed a history as possible.

A person who cannot remember his past, who does not know his history, is a person who literally does not know who he is. Every once in a while we read about an amnesia victim, a person who has lost his memory and therefore does not know who he is. We feel very sorry for such a person, and we try to help him recover his past and thus his identity.

What is true of individuals is no less true of entire communities, of families, tribes, and nations. The study of history is rightly stressed in our schools because it helps us discover who we are. Since we are human beings the study of every aspect of human history, of every aspect of our human past, contributes to our sense of identity, to our understanding of who we are.

Thus if we want to understand a religious community, we will

have to study its history. It is the history that is the clue to the
identity of a religious community as well as of an individual. It is
therefore not surprising that the Augsburg Confession in its first
article relates the people who want to identify themselves through
this document to the past.

The Augsburg Confession was supposed to answer the question,
"Who are you Lutherans, anyway?" It began the answer by relating
the subscriber to the Christian past. "We unanimously hold and
teach, in accordance with the decree of the Council of Nicaea, that
there is one divine essence, which is called and which is truly God,
and that there are three persons in this one divine essence, equal in
power and alike eternal: God the Father, God the Son, God the
Holy Spirit" (*The Book of Concord,* p. 27).

Since the signers of the document were not theologians it is
doubtful that they had a much clearer idea of the exact meaning
of this technical theological language than most of the readers
of this chapter. The mayor and council of Reutlingen who signed
the Confession were theologically no more sophisticated than the
mayor and council of Iowa City. Francis, Duke of Lüneburg,
would probably have replied with a loud and well-meaning
"Gesundheit" had anybody mentioned *"homoousios"* in his presence.

Still, signing this document was not a meaningless gesture. Especially this first article, with its references to ancient creeds and its
listing and rejection of ancient and long-forgotten heresies, helped
to identify the supporters of the Reformation as a part of the classic
Christian tradition. It helped to identify them and to tell who they
really were. The signers did not suffer from theological amnesia—
they knew their ancestry and honored it.

The Augsburg Confession raises in the first article the problem
of religious amnesia, which is still prominent in our time. We live
in an age in which many people associated with the Christian
church, both theologians and laymen, believe that we establish
relevance to our time by forgetting or at least ignoring the past.
To be modern means to these advocates of absolute relevancy to

ignore anything that originated before 1945 or even 1960 or whatever the magic year might be. We will conquer the future for the church, so they say, by ignoring the past. This theology of amnesia is, of course, the most irrelevant theology possible. If you don't know who you are yourself, you cannot be anything to anybody.

To be modern is not to forget the past, but to use it creatively for the present. The great modern composers are people who have studied the past with great care and utilized it creatively for their own artistic expression; this is equally true of the best modern painters or writers. What a brilliant use of the entire history of human literature is expressed in John Barth's exciting and controversial novel *Giles Goat-Boy!* Remembrance of things past is the key to every creative expression in the humanities, but theology as one of the humanities is weakened by amnesia.

Melanchthon, the author of the Augsburg Confession and one of the great classical scholars of his time, was completely aware of this fact. It is this awareness, this sense of the Christian past as the condition for the present and the truth of the future which is expressed in the first article of the Augsburg Confession.

To be faithful to the Augsburg Confession today means to utilize our past, which includes 400 more years of history since the Augsburg Confession, creatively for life in the present and the future.

Thus, instead of proclaiming some new God or no God or even the death of God, we shall try to proclaim the God of Abraham and Isaac and Jacob, the Father of our Lord Jesus Christ, the one true God, "in whom we live and move and have our being." In confessing our faith in God we are not defining him or describing him, but expressing our gratitude for our creation and preservation and all the blessings of this life. We join the chorus of Jews and Christians through the ages:

> If it had not been the Lord who was on our side, let Israel now say—if it had not been the Lord who was on our side, when men rose up against us, then they would have swallowed us up alive, when their anger was kindled against us; then the flood

would have swept us away, the torrent would have gone over us; then over us would have gone the raging waters. Blessed be the Lord, who has not given us as prey to their teeth! We have escaped as a bird from the snare of the fowlers; the snare is broken, and we escaped! Our help is in the name of the Lord, who made heaven and earth.

(Psalm 124)

Article II. Original Sin

In one of the most deeply moving plays of our time, Arthur Miller uses his own tortured experience with the late Marilyn Monroe, one of America's great sex-symbols, to tell us that we all, without exception, live *After the Fall*.

There is not one of us, he says, who is not guilty. Quentin, a lawyer and the hero of this play, says in connection with a visit to the site of a Nazi concentration camp: "Who can be innocent again on this mountain of skulls? I tell you what I know. My brothers died here—but my brothers built this place, our hearts have cut these stones" (A. Miller, *After the Fall*, pp. 161 f.).

Since an understanding of the Christian faith depends upon the realization that all men, without exception, are guilty, Arthur Miller's *After the Fall* can be of greater help to most people than the entire so-called "Radical Theology" or "New Morality," which tries to avoid this central issue of human existence.

The trouble is that if you don't realize you are sick, you are not likely to go to a physician, you will not take your medicine, and you will not avoid the things that cause your illness! The diagnosis of illness is the first step toward a possible cure. The Augsburg Confession asserts that all men "are born in sin. That is to say, they are without fear of God, are without trust in God, and are concupiscent" (*The Book of Concord*, p. 29).

15

This assertion has many important implications. If we take it seriously we realize that the troubles in the world, in our own country, in our family, and in our own heart cannot be simply blamed on others. We all share in the responsibility for the strife and suffering that surround us everywhere.

In international relations this means that we must avoid the notion that all conflicts between nations are the struggle of the "good guys" (our side) against the "bad guys" (our enemies). While this realization may be disappointing to those who see international conflicts as if they were a television program where heroes and villains can be clearly recognized by the color of their hats, it does bring one great advantage: We need not demand total surrender of our opponents. We can accept negotiation and compromise, for we know that *all* men—including ourselves—are born in sin.

Accepting the idea of original sin can also help us in domestic politics, because it permits us to see all conflict as arising between sinful human beings. Every election is not a foretaste of Armageddon, and angels and devils are not candidates in our political campaigns. Our world is totally a human one.

Perhaps the greatest significance of original sin is in our daily work and in our family life. If we accept the fact of original sin and realize that we are all affected by it, we should be able to face our own responsibility for the conflicts that confront us at work and at home. In the disagreements between merchants and customers, employers and employees, teachers and students, policemen and citizens, husbands and wives, parents and children—in all these conflicts the Augsburg Confession reminds us that all of us are "born with sin, that is without fear of God and with concupiscence." If we keep this in mind we should be able to give a little in our daily quarrels because we will remember that we all live "after the fall"; our pretended innocence is a fraud and a delusion.

For nobody is this insight more important than for those of us who regularly go to church and consider ourselves pillars of our community. For such people it is very easy to become like the

Pharisees of Jesus' time and glory in our own superiority over the "real sinners": the shiftless drifters, the dirty and ignorant, the irresponsible and unproductive.

When we feel superior because of our economic, social, or moral achievements we must remind ourselves that *all* men are sinners. In fact our avoidance of the more obvious and socially disapproved sins might lull us into a false security about our actual situation. Against this false sense of security the Augsburg Confession offers a defense.

There is one other point to notice about this article of the Augsburg Confession. It asserts that man cannot "be justified before God by his own strength or reason."

It is hard to imagine anybody in the 16th century believing that men had the power to save themselves. Most of them couldn't read; they didn't even have aspirin to reduce the pain of a simple headache. A good horse was their fastest means of transportation, and their life expectancy was very short indeed. Man's strength and reason were not very impressive.

What was only a minor problem in the 16th century, however, has grown into the most important theological problem of the last third of the 20th century. We are all tempted to believe that we can save ourselves. Through science in its various forms and applications we think we will be able to abolish all the old problems of man—ignorance, sickness, hunger, and strife. Some even hope that we might be able to defeat death.

We can undoubtedly make a far better case today for our "own strength and reason" than those pitiful savages in the forests of 16th century Germany. Nevertheless, it is exactly because of our apparent successes in developing our "strength and reason" that the Augsburg Confession is so important for us. We tend to forget that as long as we are without the "fear of God" and with concupiscence—that is, wanting everything for ourselves—that the more power we have and the more intelligent we are, the more dangerous we become to ourselves and to one another.

A stupid, selfish, and angry man on a horse is checked by the intelligence and equanimity of the animal. The same man in a 300-horsepower car is a mortal threat to everybody including himself. Some of the crimes committed in our time by individuals and by communities are possible only because of the power that our intellect has given us. Nothing, then, is more important to modern men than the humbling realization that they all live after the fall and that they cannot save themselves. In the 16th century, when people had little power, they could perhaps afford to ignore this fact. Today, just because we have so much power, ignorance of the sinful human situation is not bliss but death.

Article III. The Son of God

In every line of work the most important condition for success is a good model; we have to have a pattern, a blueprint, or a plan in order to build anything. This is as true for the dressmaker as for the designer of an interplanetary space vehicle. Doing things without some sort of plan is merely "fooling around."

While we are aware of this need in all the little things we do, we often forget that it applies also to our life as a whole. There are many people who either do not have a plan for their life or else cannot decide which of the many available options to choose. Some people just "fool around"; they take the raw material of their life, the time and the talents given to them, and just saw a little here and nail a little there. When they finally try seriously to follow some pattern there is no more time left and their talents are wasted.

Such people are often very gifted; because they are so talented they can improvise successfully and often do not become aware of the lack of direction in their lives until there isn't much time left. Having limited abilities often gives one a real advantage—you learn very soon to use what talent you have in an orderly fashion if you want to accomplish anything at all.

But even if you know that you ought to have a plan for your life the question arises—which one should you use? Like the proverbial donkey who starved between two equally luscious bales of hay because he could not decide which to eat first, many people simply cannot decide among the different patterns of life that are available to them.

What are some of these alternatives? You can, for example, build your life around pleasure. You can design everything in order to achieve the greatest amount of pleasure for yourself. Don Giovanni, the hero of Mozart's great opera, exemplifies this type of planning. *Playboy* Magazine offers a somewhat dimwitted version of this approach to Americans, and sales indicate that it is a popular design—though there is always the hope that people buy the magazine to look at the pictures rather than to read its turgid "philosophy."

Or you can plan your life for power. It is quite possible to design a life for the achievement of power. Hitler might be a good model of this approach. There are people all over the world, from Viet Nam to the U.S.A., who still admire him. In politics and in business there are many people whose life is clearly designed for the accumulation of power.

It is also possible to design a life around the achievement of knowledge. Here knowledge becomes not merely a means to an end, like power or pleasure, but an end in itself. There are people who just want to know, even if this knowledge makes no practical difference whatsoever. They want to *know* the meaning of Etruscan inscriptions, they want to *know* the age of the universe, not because such knowledge is useful but because knowledge is the purpose of their life. Perhaps Dr. Faust, the hero of Goethe's tragedy, is the best model of this approach to life.

There are many other possibilities, but the Augsburg Confession asserts in its third article that Jesus is the Christ, or in other words God's model for the kind of human beings he wants us to be. Man is not merely "an individual (genus *Homo,* family Hominidae, class Mammalia) of the highest type of animal existing or known to have existed, differing from other high types of animals, especially in his extraordinary mental development" (Webster). This may be very true, but it is trivial compared to the assertion that Jesus, the Christ, is God's man. The model for man's life is not Don Giovanni or Hitler or Faust, and the key to the meaning of life is not Java Man, Neanderthal Man or Cro-Magnon Man, but Jesus alone.

The Augsburg Confession asserts that God's clue to the meaning of "man" is the Son of Mary, "who was truly born, suffered, was crucified, died and was buried" but at the same time God's chosen model.

There is one important distinction between models like Don Giovanni, Hitler, or Faust, and Jesus, the Christ. We all try to imitate our models to the best of our ability. They are out there in front of us, inspiring us by their perfection, urging us on to do as well. Achieving the perfection of our human models is completely up to us, for the models themselves have no active power to help us become like them. The situation is completely different with God's model. As the Augsburg Confession states it, "Through the Holy Spirit he may sanctify, purify, strengthen, and comfort all who believe in him, that he may bestow on them life and every grace and blessing, and that he may protect and defend them against the devil and against sin" (*B. of C.,* p. 30).

In very simple language this means that God's model for man has the power not only to inspire men to imitate him but actually to change those who trust in him. God's becoming man means that not only do we know now what a real human being is like, not only do we know what kind of human beings we ought to be, but Jesus also actively transforms us, if we trust in him, into the kind of persons we are actually designed to be. This is what it means to say that he has "dominion over all creatures." Jesus not only asks us to be his kind of human beings, but he also enables us to become what he asks us to be if we only trust him.

All this seems particularly important in our time, for three reasons. First, we have today many more models to choose from than people in other ages had. Possibilities which men in other ages never dreamed of are commonplace today. Second, we have much more power to change men ourselves by means of biochemical, genetic, and psychological control techniques. This means, however, that we must have some model, otherwise this whole scientific operation can become a very dangerous "fooling around." Finally, in our world power, pleasure, and knowledge are so very important that people despair of truly imitating Jesus by their own efforts. This may have seemed possible in ancient Palestine or medieval Europe, but in our age it seems just too hard to do. It may, indeed, be too hard for us, but the Augsburg Confession reminds us that he who is the model also has the power to transform us according to his plan if we only will let him.

Since we have to choose some model, which shall it be?

Article IV. Justification

If you ever get into a discussion with Europeans about the advisability of adopting children, you will soon discover that most of them are far more hesitant and skeptical about this practice than is the typical American. The reason for this is the much greater emphasis in the minds of most Europeans upon the importance of heredity. Americans, in contrast, tend to stress the importance of environment.

In very basic terms, this means that most Europeans emphasize the power of your ancestors (your genes, to be technical) to determine the kind of person you are going to be. This makes adoption a very risky business indeed. Most Americans have much more confidence in the power of the example and teaching of parents and teachers, of education and culture, to form a child into a particular kind of human being.

It is for this reason that the European Sigmund Freud, with his great emphasis upon the decisive influences of the experiences of early infancy and childhood on the personality of the adult, developed a far greater following in America than in his own heredity-oriented Europe. The very notion of a hereditary "nobility," so prominent for centuries in most parts of the world, including Europe, is alien and a little offensive to most Americans. We believe that "all men are created equal," and any distinction made among the genetic heritages of different individuals offends our sense of democratic justice. We have not gone as far as some Russians, who simply denied certain genetic laws as subversive to communist ideas, but we certainly do not like these hereditary advantages and disadvantages with which some people are supposedly born.

But actually it does not matter too much whether you believe in the determining power of heredity or the determining power of environment, for in either case, by the time you are ready to take your place in life, either or both of them have been at work to make you the kind of person you are—and you are stuck with the outcome. According to hereditary or environmental determinists, you can do little or nothing about it; you simply must learn to live with the results.

What both of these views have in common is their obsession with the past. They look at life as the gradual unfolding of a pattern or a picture that has actually been determined earlier. This is the notion of "fate" or "destiny" so prevalent in the minds of many men. Nothing we can do can change our fate. The harder we try to escape, the faster we fulfill our destiny. We are determined by the past—whether this is understood as the Indian *Karma* or a Freudian *trauma,* the genetic code of modern biochemistry or the inexorable laws of communist dialectical materialism.

In the language of the street it means that you know "You can't beat City Hall." Just as the games of chance in a casino are so rigged that in the long run the house always wins and the customer always loses, so the roulette wheel of life is so rigged that man always loses. Even if you catch the big fish, like the hero in Hemingway's *The Old Man and the Sea,* by the time you get it home the sharks have eaten it to a skeleton. The past determines both the present and the future; the dice are loaded against us, and even if we think we win, we lose.

The doctrine of justification by grace through faith, of which the fourth article of the Augsburg Confession speaks, is a frontal attack against this entire way of thinking and living. Neither our heredity nor our environment—or in theological terms, neither our original sin nor our own merits or works—determine our destiny, but only God's grace.

What really matters, says the Augsburg Confession, is that God loves you and that he has shown his love for you and all men in Jesus who is the Christ. "For his sake our sin is forgiven and righteousness and eternal life are given to us." Not your heredity or your environment, not your good or evil works of the past determine your future, but God's love does—if you will only let it.

Few people realize what an utterly revolutionary assertion this is. It actually goes against all our customary religion. The notion that we are saved by our good works is probably the most universally held belief of men. It is the "common faith" of all people regardless of their pretended religion or lack of it. It can be reduced to the slogan, "God loves good people and hates bad people." Or, "Everybody is a self-made man, but the successful ones are willing to admit it." Thus, being "good" we can assure ourselves of God's love for us.

The revolutionary assertion of Article Four is that God loves all people because *he* is good, not because we are. It is for this reason that he made himself known to us in Jesus Christ and wants us to be like him. And he wants it not because it is good for him but because it is good for us.

Certainly men can live without God, but without him our life will be meaningless and empty, coming from nowhere and going nowhere, doomed by fate and death. Faith is not doing God a favor—it is doing ourselves the greatest favor possible. God is what he is without us, the same yesterday, today, and forever. But without him we are nothing. God is not dead, but men are dying.

There is, however, one great danger in this powerful idea of justification. When righteousness before God on the grounds of "our own merits, works, or satisfactions" is thrown out the front door, it tends to creep in the back door. People who do not believe they have a claim on God because of their good works often think they have a claim on him because of their good faith. They think that faith is some contest where they receive an award for holding things to be true which they really consider highly improbable or unlikely. Faith, then, becomes a new kind of good work, believing a long list of fairly unbelievable assertions. The more unbelievable they seem, the greater the faith of those who believe them.

In the Augsburg Confession, faith is one thing only: trusting completely in Jesus, the Christ. "Now if a man does a piece of work, his wages are not 'counted' as a favour; they are paid as debt. But if without any work to his credit he simply puts his faith in him who acquits the guilty, then his faith is indeed 'counted as righteousness' " (Romans 4:5, *NEB*).

Your heredity may have been awful, your environment degrading, and your own performance as a human being deplorable, but this is all past. You do not have to live from the past. You are allowed to live for the future. Justification means that God has given you a new start.

Article V. The Office of the Ministry

Have you ever spent some time with a man or woman who is madly in love with somebody? If so, you may remember it as one of the most boring episodes of your life. The reason is obvious: People in love often want to talk incessantly about the object of their affection. Whatever effort you may make to turn the conversation to sports or politics or even the weather, they will invariably return to the woman or man who is the center of all their interest.

Furthermore, people who are in love have the tendency to want everybody else to share this experience. They are forever plotting to have a certain young lady of their acquaintance meet a certain bachelor in the hope that something might develop and these two people may also come to experience this wonderful reality of love.

There are certain experiences which are simply so powerful that they make anybody who has had them into an advertising agent. He has to talk about them.

In the same way, it is not surprising that knowing the good news "that we have a gracious God, not by our own merits but by the merit of Christ" produces the desire to make this message known. In fact, according to the Augsburg Confession such knowledge results in the office of the ministry, the obligation to proclaim the good news of God's love to everybody.

There are two dangers in this ministry of proclamation: clericalism and enthusiasm. We should look at both of them. In the 16th century clericalism was represented by certain branches of the religious institution who were willing to be religious in your stead. You paid them a fee to pray for you and say masses on your behalf. Just as a lawyer would take care of your legal obligations (and the better the lawyer the less you would be bothered by legal problems) so the cleric would take care of your religious obligations with a minimum of bother to you. Turning your faith over to a professional group of religious experts to take care of it for you is clericalism. While the Reformation was in part a protest against 16th century clericalism, the problem remained and is still very real in our time.

There are many church members who think of the minister as the "symbolic Christian." Depending on the denominational emphasis, they expect him to feel, believe, or do what they think a Christian ought to feel, believe, or do. He discharges this responsibility for them, and for that they are willing to pay him a meager salary.

Some stress the believing more. This may mean that while practically all the members who went to school think the world is many million years old they expect the minister to believe it was created six thousand years ago. Others stress the doing more. Thus while practically the whole adult congregation either smokes or drinks they expect the minister to be a non-smoking total abstainer for them. This is clericalism pure and simple—even if the denomination in question doesn't have a professional clergy and the minister works in a machine shop to earn most of his living.

The Augsburg Confession insists that the office of the ministry exists so that people may come to faith. It exists for the sake of people, as a means to an end. It is the office of the "Gospel and the sacraments. Through these as through means [God] gives the Holy

Spirit who works faith, when and where he pleases, in those who hear the Gospel." The office of the ministry exists for the sake of people. Apart from its service to people, apart from its effect on those who receive the sacrament and hear the word, it has no significance at all. This is why Luther abolished both services that were held without a congregation present and communion where nobody communed.

But there is another danger to the office of the ministry, namely, when sincerity takes the place of the external word of the Gospel. We all have heard the expression, "I don't care what you believe as long as you are sincere." In the 16th century there were some very sincere people whom Luther called *Schwärmer,* or "Enthusiasts," who substituted their own visions for the external word of the Gospel. Luther's emphasis upon the external word of the Gospel seemed to them mechanical and insincere. They felt that they had direct access to God by means of their mystical experience and were not dependent on the witness of the Prophets, Evangelists, and Apostles.

The office of the ministry, as an office of the Gospel and the sacraments, is a safeguard against similar temptations in our time. The proclamation of the church is not what somebody happens to feel strongly about—be it ever so interesting. It is defined by the Gospel, the good news of what God has done in Jesus, the Christ. The Augsburg Confession asserts that neither the fact that a man is ordained nor that he is sincere guarantees the reliability of his message as a Christian statement; his proclamation depends only on the external word of the Gospel. We live in an age when many ordained clergymen, even bishops (who are obviously terribly sincere, candid, and honest) write a lot of sincere nonsense. When people say, "He is a bishop, it must be true," or, "It must be true, he is so sincere," the Augsburg Confession reminds us to look for the external word of the Gospel.

The position or sincerity of a person does not guarantee the truth of his ministry, but the Gospel does. Thus when you first heard from the lips of your mother or perhaps your Sunday school teacher the news of the love and grace of God, they participated in the office of the ministry; and when you tell of this same love to others you participate as well.

The setting of one's ministry also doesn't matter. Some people never listen to anything they hear in church; they are so conditioned that they turn off their minds when they enter the building and keep them turned off until they leave again. Some of these same people are willing to listen over a glass of beer in a tavern. It is the exercise of the office of the ministry to talk to people where they are willing to listen. This is apparently what Jesus did—even if it meant he had to feed them too. Perhaps we can still learn something from him about the office of the ministry.

Article VI. The New Obedience

What makes a person act in a considerate, helpful, and loving manner toward other people? This is a question continually faced by every family and school, every community and nation. The very future of the human race seems to depend on our ability to find an answer which will actually work.

Some say that people are very much like animals, that they can be trained or conditioned to become considerate, loving, and helpful. Those who see human behavior as an "animal act" in which human beings are trained like dogs or horses to do tricks are themselves divided between those who emphasize the stick and those who stress candy as the motivating device. Some believe people will act most responsibly when they are afraid of punishment, while others claim that the hope of a reward is the more effective motive. In either case, though, both parties say that obedience is a matter of training. The good life is a form of obedience to rules, and these rules are learned in the manner in which animals learn in the psychology laboratory.

To put it bluntly, these people say that the clue to human behavior is the rat. If we shall ever understand why laboratory rats act the way they do, we shall also understand what makes people tick.

It would be perverse to deny that there is some truth in this observation. No doubt there are some fascinating similarities between the behavior of human beings and that of rats. I have been told that this goes so far that in the laboratory you can produce an alcoholic rat. If you frustrate the animal sufficiently, that is, confuse and irritate it so that it does not know what to do, and then offer it a choice between pure water and a solution containing alcohol, it will prefer the alcoholic beverage. Such similarities are indeed impressive. Much modern mass-psychology, called "advertising" when we do it in the West and "brainwashing" when the Russians and Chinese do it, is based on this single claim: that you can condition people to do what you want them to do, to bring forth "good works." They may then buy the soap you want them to buy, shout the slogan you want them to shout, or even kill the people you want them to kill. In any case, human beings are trainable.

The Augsburg Confession refuses to take sides between the advocates of conditioning through punishment or reward, for it claims that there is a third possible motive for human action. In Article Six the Augsburg Confession states, "Our churches also teach that *this faith* is *bound* to bring forth good fruits." It is important to note here that only a certain kind of faith is believed to result in good fruits. This means that not every faith will do. The Confession does not say "faith is bound to bring forth good fruits," but rather "*this* faith is bound to bring forth good fruits." In other words, when people believe that they are received into God's favor and that their sins are forgiven for Christ's sake they will spontaneously do good works.

The specific content of faith is apparently very important in the Confession. I can have faith in my own superiority and as a result become an impossible bore and a threat to other human beings. This is the story of Dostoevsky's Raskolnikov, who believed he could kill a certain pawnbroker of his acquaintance because

Raskolnikov thought himself a superior being and the pawnbroker inferior and worthless. I can have faith in the superiority of my race, the infallibility of my church, the manifest destiny of my nation, or the victory of my class—and all this may only result in evil works, that is, suffering and disaster for me and everybody else. The Augsburg Confession does not say, "any faith produces good fruits." It does say that if you truly believe God loves you and all other men unconditionally, a life of love and service will result. If you really believe that your sins are forgiven, you are enabled to forgive those who have offended and hurt you

This method is not the way you train animals. If you want to teach a dog a trick you reward him *after* he has rolled over, stood on his hind legs, or barked. If you give him his dog-candy first he won't do a thing. The Augsburg Confession claims that God treats us like men—not like dogs. He forgives us our sins and shows us his love first and expects us then to forgive and show love to others.

Does it work? You are both the "guinea pig" and the "judge" in this divine experiment, designed to show that men are different. The Augsburg Confession claims that God wants us to do the works commanded by him—but he wants us to do them because he loves us and we love him, and because we want to share this love with those who need it. Can we live human lives of gratitude and love, or must we live lives based on fear of punishment or hope for reward? Our Confession stresses man's humanity and pleads for faith active in love rather than divine love as a reward for man's good works.

Article Six makes another point. The deeds that flow from our appreciation of God's love are "good works commanded by God." Here the Confession makes a distinction between all those "religious deeds" that men have invented to please God and those deeds which God has commanded to serve the neighbor. The history of religion is full of lists of peculiar actions, from the sublime to the ridiculous, which men have devised to impress God.

Some have sacrificed their first-born sons, others have given up buttons for hooks to fasten their clothes. Some have grown long hair and beards, while others have shaved off every hair on their body. All this is foolishness and worse according to the Augsburg Confession. The "new obedience," which flows from knowing that God loves us and has forgiven us our sins, expresses itself in acts of love which really help the neighbor. The "good works" commanded by God are to feed the hungry, to clothe the naked, to heal the sick, to comfort the sad, and to proclaim good news to the poor. In this way we show the "new obedience" which is that of loving children, not frightened rats.

Article VII. The Church

During the 19th century distinguished British writers would occasionally come to the United States to give lectures. Often these lectures insulted the adoring "natives" for their uncouth and primitive ways and for their obvious inability to use the Queen's English properly. For delivering these insults the lecturers were very well paid and allowed to return to England full of fantastic tales of the American Wild West.

When reading the books published by some contemporary theologians dealing with the church and its many glaring shortcomings, one is reminded a little of these 19th century performances by sneering visiting firemen from abroad. Most of the books ridiculing the church in our time are written by men who are on some ecclesiastical payroll and collect their royalties from doting church members who apparently love to be insulted and who seem to like to pay for the privilege. Those people who are frankly hostile to the Christian church and its message do not bother to read these debunking efforts—they couldn't care less. It is the faithful church members who seem to get some perverse satisfaction out of receiving such loveless and careless attacks.

Does it really do people any good to be constantly told how stupid and irrelevant they are? Is this how one best encourages them to act intelligently and with concern for present needs? Since many of these disdainful authors are educators, one is tempted to ask, "Is this the way you educate students who are not doing well? Are ridicule and contempt the most persuasive device to bring about changes or to encourage people to act responsibly?"

Whatever their answer, the Augsburg Confession does not take such a negative approach. There were certainly many things wrong with the church in the 16th century; in later sections of the Confession these "abuses" are listed and described. But our article follows a more positive approach by constructively stating what the church is. It is eternal: "One holy Christian church will be and remain forever."

Many people in the 16th century were worried about all the new religious ideas coming from the universities. Some said bitterly, "Is nothing sacred these days, can't we even trust the monks?" They felt that they were losing all the firm ground under their feet. But to all of them, both the followers of the new ideas and the defenders of the old, our Confession proclaims that God's church will be and remain forever. Keep cool, friends, the church is God's establishment, "and the gates of hell shall not prevail against it."

Such a proclamation tends to put everything else into perspective. Only on the basis of this confession is a constructive criticism of the church possible. If you cannot confidently confess the steadfast love of God for his church, any further talk about the church is a waste of time. Only because the church is God's eternal people does it make sense even to criticize it and to try to reform it. If this were not the case, you could only bury it like a dead horse or junk it like a broken-down car. If a criticism of the church does not show this confidence that the Augsburg Confession so clearly demonstrates, it is useless.

Then the Confession continues that the church "is the assembly of all believers among whom the Gospel is preached in its purity and the holy sacraments are administered according to the Gospel." The church is people who trust Jesus, the Christ. Not institutions, not even theology constitutes the church, but people who have faith in Christ.

This does not mean that institutions aren't important. But they are important only as means to an end. Churches as institutions with buildings and church councils, Sunday schools, and even kitchens exist so that people may hear the Gospel. If they don't contribute to this end, they should be closed, and other institutions developed which will do the job. There is nothing holy about the congregational system which we have been using in America. It is no more and no less holy than the Episcopal system that so many Europeans have used. The only proper question is, "Does the system we have help God's people to hear the Gospel?" You are the judge. If our institutions don't do the job they are designed to do, we'll have to change them. Institutions are dispensable; they are only tools.

But what about theology? Isn't our theology eternal? Theology is only a way to explain what God has done for the world in Jesus the Christ so that people can understand this message. Incomprehensible theology is not theology at all. It is only a highly developed indoor sport played by certain theologians for their own edification. It is neither eternal nor important; it is a waste of time. It has as much in common with the proper task of theology as building a ship in a bottle has in common with the proper task of maritime transportation. Anybody who does this sort of thing should do it on evenings and weekends on his own time, and pump gasoline for a living.

But since there are all kinds of people, we need many varieties of theology in order to communicate the Gospel to all of them. We need simple theologies for simple people and more subtle theologies for more complicated people. But a theology which only theologians can understand is a fraud and justifies demands for a new theology, or at least new theologians. Theology for theology's sake is a joke.

Finally our article states that "it is sufficient for the true unity of the Christian church that the Gospel be preached in conformity with a pure understanding of it and that the sacraments be administered in accordance with the divine Word."

One of the most exciting aspects of our age is the new ecumenical spirit. Christians seem to have rediscovered their sense of belonging together: their unity in Christ. We are learning to think of other Christians as brothers rather than as enemies or heretics. But in this wonderful new mood we should remember that the source of our unity as Christians is not our good feeling for one another or even our brilliant plans for a great and all-inclusive church; we are joined only in the Gospel of Christ.

The Augsburg Confession states that where this Gospel of grace and forgiveness is preached there is unity *now*, even if institutions and ceremonies differ. Thus Christian unity is reached by way of the Gospel, not by some detour around it. As we try to discover the unity that God has given his church, we must concentrate on this Gospel; even the best paved and broadest detour will only keep us from reaching the goal.

Article VIII. What the Church Is

The oldest and most persistent attack upon the church is based on the fact that so many who claim to be Christians neither look, nor talk, nor act like it. In other words, there are lots of hypocrites in the church. When somebody came to Dwight L. Moody with this complaint and told him that he would not join the church since there were so many hypocrites in it, Moody is said to have replied, "Don't let that bother you, there is always room for one more." The only thing that is even more hypocritical than hypocrites in the church is people who stay away from churches because they claim they are so much better. It is hard to beat this attitude for sheer unmitigated hypocrisy.

Once we have granted the fact that "in this life many hypocrites and evil persons are mingled with believers," what does this tell us about the church? The most obvious implication clearly stated in this article of the Confession is that the validity of the Gospel does not depend on the sincerity or moral purity of those who transmit it to us. The Gospel is true because it is God's message, not because the minister or Sunday school teacher happens to be a good man. But while this seems self-evident, many people claim to have lost faith in the Gospel and even in God because of some unfortunate experience with a representative of the church. Yet nobody would say the truth of the American Constitution depends on the personal honesty and integrity of a congressman or even the President of the United States. We would rather claim that just because of the human weakness of politicians the truths embodied in the system of checks and balances of the Constitution are especially important. Just because a congressman puts his wife or mistress on the payroll, we do not start burning the Constitution; instead, we look for remedies which the Constitution offers against corrupt politicians.

It is indeed most desirable that the people who proclaim the Gospel represent it well—but the truth of the message does not depend on the competence or integrity of the messenger. This is the first lesson of this article.

The second lesson is no less important, though not quite as obvious. This article suggests that the church ought to be inclusive rather than exclusive. They say about certain banks that you can get a loan from them only if you can prove that you do not really need the money. Some churches act similarly; they are interested only in good people, and they offer salvation only to those who already know that they are saved.

But if you know that "in this life many false Christians, hypocrites, and even open sinners remain among the godly," you do not have to be so fussy. Since the integrity of the church depends on the holiness of her Lord and the truth of her Gospel, not on the holiness and sincerity of her members, you can take chances. It is enough that people want to stand with this Lord and hear and proclaim this message even in an imperfect and halting way to accept them gladly. Their motives may be mixed, they may even come for very foolish or very selfish reasons, but these reasons and motives can be transformed by the Lord of the church so that such people may become eloquent witnesses to the Gospel. The church is not a holy club for the pure and sinless; it is a hospital for those who are sick with sin. Many people came to Jesus in Palestine for selfish and foolish reasons. For some it was a last chance. "What can I lose?" the lepers and blind said. "There may be a free meal in it," thought some who followed him into the wilderness. And out of this mixed bag of people some stayed and became disciples. Our Confession encourages us to take chances on people, to see them as Jesus would see them: sick, hungry, and lost, but children of God in search of a home. "Don't make human rules to exclude people whom God includes," says our Confession.

Nevertheless, we always tend to make such rules. Some are intellectual, some are moral, and recently the rules have become increasingly financial. There are many people in America who are simply too poor to afford the ministry of a respectable church. They do not own their own homes, they are jobless, or they have the wrong family background; therefore they do not pass our "means test" for church membership. We might have included them had they been hypocrites or even open sinners—but if they are poor and ignorant they are out. That is where we often draw the line.

This is why the final lesson from our article is so important, for it suggests that the church is always in need of reformation. We remember Luther and the posting of the 95 Theses. We hear a lot about the Reformation of the 16th century, but it will not do us much good if we do not learn that the Reformation must continue. Because the church consists of forgiven sinners, it will always develop sinful tendencies that have to be repaired. What Luther did in 1517 is not enough. If we count ourselves faithful to Luther, we must help reform the church today where it is weak and failing. Luther asked himself: What interferes with the proclamation of the Gospel of God's gracious forgiveness of sins in Wittenberg today? Because he thought the way indulgences were peddled subverted the Gospel, he spoke out.

What interferes with the Gospel of God's gracious forgiveness of sins where you live? I am sure it is not the sale of indulgences. But then what is it? You'd better find out, and then do something about it.

Article IX. Baptism

The entire Christian church has at times been facetiously divided into two groups: "the Lord's Army" and "the Lord's Navy." In this division, those who practice believer's baptism and immersion are, of course, "the Lord's Navy." Those who practice infant baptism and use relatively little water for the purpose are "the Lord's Army." The discussion about the significance of Baptism in back of this distinction is particularly fervent in America, where "Baptists" represent the largest Protestant denominational family. But in spite of the ardor that has characterized this controversy one would have to say that a very real and basic misunderstanding has made the argument over baptism contribute little to the enlightenment of the participants. The important fact is that the parties in the argument are not really talking about the same thing. For those who practice "believer's baptism" the rite is primarily an act of public confession. For those who practice "infant baptism" it is a sacrament, that is, "an action appointed by Christ, in which the general promise of the Gospel concerning the forgiveness of sins for Christ's sake is applied and sealed to an individual in the use of an external element."

If Baptism is an act of public confession on the part of the person being baptized, it is silly or even absurd to baptize infants. A week-old baby cannot make a public confession of faith; everybody must admit that. But if Baptism is a means of grace in which the promise of the Gospel is applied and sealed to an individual, then it does not really matter how old the person is to whom this seal is applied. It is then a sign conveying God's grace and forgiveness, and does not depend for its value on the understanding of the recipient. One can leave money to a child which may benefit the child greatly long before he understands the use and significance of money. Or even more accurately, you can kiss and cuddle a baby and make him feel your love and protection long before the baby will have any rational understanding of love and protection. The reality of the love does not depend on our intellectual comprehension of it.

When the Augsburg Confession, therefore, says that Baptism is necessary for salvation, it points to two very important facts of the Christian life: (1) God's love is necessary for salvation—and Baptism is one major experience of this love. (2) God's love comes to us long before we can even begin to understand what it means. And our understanding will be inadequate as long as we live in this world and "see through a mirror dimly," as the Apostle Paul puts it.

It is a consistent note—indeed, the theme of the Augsburg Confession—that God offers us his grace freely and without any merit on our part. He offers us his grace because he is good, not because we are. He has loved us before we were even conceived or born. Baptism expresses this unconditional character of God's love. It shows how God reaches out to us before we were even aware of him.

Baptism denies any notion that God's love is aroused by our moral goodness or intellectual understanding or even our mystical experience of love. A small infant does not do evil or good. It acts on the level of immediacy, smiling when warm and full and crying when cold or hungry. Yet God loves these children and takes them into his family before they can have any inkling of morality.

Similarly, a baby does not have the slightest understanding of theology. It is really totally ignorant. Yet God loves the child in spite of its complete ignorance of the basic facts of the Christian faith. To the best of our knowledge, a baby has no mystical experiences of God's presence and love, but regardless of the baby's inability to give a time or date for his conversion or enlightenment, God loves the child.

Baptism teaches us who are often so proud of our moral achievements or intellectual comprehension of theology or our religious experiences and visions that none of these things establish a claim on God. God has claimed us in Baptism long before we could claim him. We can love him because he has loved us first.

The very comforting aspect of this message of Baptism is that achievements or failures do not really determine our relationship to God. God loves us because he is love and not because of our moral, intellectual, or mystical accomplishments. This is what Jesus tells us today when we read his words to those disciples who tried to prevent parents from bringing small children to him: "Let the children come to me; do not try to stop them; for the kingdom of God belongs to such as these" (Mark 10:14, *NEB*). "Such as these" are people who let go of their claims on God and let God claim them, touch them, and baptize them.

The way in which God claims us in Baptism also reminds us that our belonging to God does not ever depend on our full comprehension of what this may mean. Some may think that while for little children the relationship which God has established in Baptism is sufficient, adults have to comprehend God and his plan for them. But Jesus said to the disciples when the infants were brought to him, "I tell you, whoever does not accept the kingdom of God like a child will never enter it." In relation to God we always remain like children. We never fully comprehend God's plan or purpose. Here and there we may get a glimpse of it—there may be times when we see our part in it quite clearly—but these are only fleeting moments. Even for a Moses or an Isaiah, a Peter or a Paul, such clarity was the exception rather than the rule.

The effort to understand God, to place him in the cage of one or the other of our logical systems, is always bound to fail. In our time many people are desperately trying to cut God down to size so that he will fit into our modern world view, but it just will not work. It is like trying to catch the sunshine in a butterfly net—the attempt never succeeds, and those who try hardest make fools of themselves. The reason is very simple—we are closest to God when we respond like children to a loving father, accepting his love trustingly and gladly even when his actions bewilder us.

When the Augsburg Confession asserts so very bluntly that "Baptism is necessary for salvation" it really asserts that God's love is necessary to salvation. Baptism is the seal of God's love at the very beginning of our life. All that is left to do is to learn how to use this overwhelming gift, but that always takes a lifetime for both God's Army and Navy.

Article X. The Lord's Supper

In the long history of Christianity the Lord's Supper has been one of the major sources of controversy. From the difficulties in Corinth described by the Apostle Paul in his first letter to the Corinthians to the current ecumenical discussions it is this overwhelming gift of the Lord of the church to his people which has ever again caused strife and confusion among them.

At first this may seem odd; indeed, some people have even questioned the value of the sacrament because it has resulted in so many divisions among Christians. Such critics, however, know very little about human nature. Among human beings the most valuable gifts always cause the greatest strife. A family may have lived peacefully for years, with only the bare necessities of life. Then some relative dies and leaves them a fortune, and immediately the arguments begin. Rather than being grateful for the new wealth, they will quarrel and bicker as never before. The very value of the inheritance has caused them to disagree.

Small wonder that the Lord's Supper has caused so many divisions. The long history of argument does not reflect the worthlessness of the gift but instead mirrors the worthlessness of the recipients, who quarrel precisely because they are dimly aware of the tremendous value of the inheritance.

As in all human controversies about gifts, the basic argument has been over who shall control it. One of the most terrible punishments which the medieval church could impose on recalcitrant rulers and people was the interdict. This meant that the sacraments—and especially the Lord's Supper—was withheld from the people who had offended the ecclesiastical dignitaries who believed that they controlled these gifts of the Lord. The Lord's Supper was a way of controlling men. Among Protestants similar customs developed. People were excluded from the Lord's Supper, or "excommunicated," even for disagreeing with the pastor or the church council on matters of church finance or geology.

But not only the "orthodox" have used this great gift of the Lord to try to control others; the "liberals" have tended in the same direction. Again and again liberal Protestants wanted to use the Lord's Supper to pretend a unity which did not really exist, or to show how much better Christians they were than those who had conscientious scruples about indiscriminate Communion services promoting causes like the welfare of the local fire department or the spiritual unity of the Council of Churches. Apparently, what all of us have in common is a tendency to use the sacrament of the Lord's Supper for our own purposes and as a means to our own ends.

The Augsburg Confession breaks into this old argument in a rather strange way. It merely states, "It is taught among us that the body and blood of Christ are really present in the Supper of our Lord under the form of bread and wine and are there distributed and received. The contrary doctrine is therefore rejected."

The argument at this point of the Confession is primarily directed against those who would reduce the Lord's Supper to a memorial service for the absent Christ. Whether there were many people in the 16th century who held such a "memorial view" of the sacrament is today hard to establish. That there are many in our time who treat Holy Communion as if it were a delayed funeral service for "poor Jesus" is hard to deny. Regardless of their theologies, many people treat Communion as if it were something sad, something depending on their own feelings for its significance and not very important anyway.

Why do so many people think of the Lord's Supper as something depressing? Partly because of the setting. The night of institution was the night in which Jesus was betrayed. But after all, Communion assures us of the eternal presence of Christ, so why be so dejected when we are about to meet the best friend we ever had?

The answer to this question is probably that for many Christians religion is something sad and depressing anyway, and Holy Communion, one of the most meaningful moments of the Christian life, becomes infected with the general attitude that religion demands a sour face and a sad heart. The Augsburg Confession, by stressing the real presence of our Savior and Lord, calls our attention to the joy of the occasion.

What about the importance of our feelings for the reality of the Lord's Supper? Here again Christians have tended to stress the mood of the recipient and not the mood of the donor; thus they have confused the issue. Many people will not participate in Communion because they are "not in the right mood," as if their mood mattered. What matters is that God loves us, not that we love him. Holy Communion is the celebration of God's love, not of man's worthiness to receive this love. Yet every year millions of Christians absent themselves from the Lord's Table because they feel not worthy to appear in his presence. On the contrary, the person who really should not show up is the person who pretends to be worthy of this gift. It is not the psychological mood of contriteness produced by man which makes the Lord's Supper important. This the Augsburg Confession states very clearly. Christ is *really* present in the Supper. This presence is his free gift of love, and not the result of our spiritual exercises.

Finally, the Lord's Supper is important. It is the central feast of the Christian church because it expresses the central fact of this faith—"that we receive forgiveness of sin and become righteous before God by grace, for Christ's sake through faith" (Article IV). Nothing illustrates the life-giving support we receive from God better than the act of eating. As Christians are fed by the bread and wine of Holy Communion they receive forgiveness of sins and life-giving power from the Christ who is present for them. He who once fed the multitudes at the shores of the Sea of Galilee is now feeding all those who come to him at the Lord's Supper. Since this food provides forgiveness of sins and a new life, it is a meal we cannot do without. Because it is so important it has been the center of much controversy. But for the same reason a healthy Christian life demands faithful participation in the Supper of our Lord. To neglect it means spiritual starvation.

Article XI. Confession

It is not unusual for religious practices neglected and almost forgotten by the original practitioners to be adopted by the outside world in a modified and non-religious way and to become very fashionable in this new form. For example, when the church gave up fasting the world took up dieting. There can be little doubt that some of the diets modern people follow are far more rigid and bring one closer to starvation than any but the most extreme fasting customs of former times.

Thus people do for their health or their beauty what they were quite unwilling to do for God or the neighbor. We do not fast, but we diet. Similarly people who do not confess their sins to God are willing to go to the psychoanalyst to tell him everything. While the religious practice of private confession and absolution has fallen into disuse among most Protestants, the practice of completely uncovering your innermost thoughts and your most secret desires to a psychoanalyst has become quite acceptable; it is even a status symbol. Having a psychoanalyst is for some people like having a stock broker or a hairdresser—it proves that they have arrived socially.

It is significant that the Augsburg Confession advocated private confession and absolution: "It is taught among us that private absolution should be retained and not allowed to fall into disuse. However, in confession it is not necessary to enumerate all trespasses and sins, for this is impossible."

Why are confession and absolution necessary? The reason is simply that all men appear to suffer from a deep sense of guilt; in order for them to live fruitful lives it is important to help them come to terms with their experience of guilt.

This sense of guilt, of course, is not necessarily what we talk about when we use the word "sin" in church. It is quite possible not to feel guilty about those things that are condemned by our particular religious group or even by society. But the universal guilt-producing experience is the tension between what we are and what we ought to be. What counts is not so much what other people think we ought to be but what we ourselves want to be according to our own standards.

It matters little that the standards may differ widely from person to person. What does matter as far as the universal experience of guilt is concerned is that we all have some standards—and that if we are honest with ourselves, we must all admit that we fail to live up to our very own standards. The good things we want to do we do not do, and the evil things we do not want to do we do.

This is experienced already by the child. None of us reaches his teens without having felt his own inadequacy. Our problem is not so much that there are certain things we cannot do which we would like to be able to do, but rather that we all have some awareness of our own abilities and also a profound sense that we are not living up to our own potential—however limited it may be. There is the little boy who would like to help his father in some building project. He would like to saw a piece of wood just right, and he knows he can do it—but it turns out badly, so he feels terrible and hates himself. There is a girl who would like to be able to bake a cake—but it collapses, so she feels that she has failed to live up to her own standards and is very angry with herself.

Moral failure—our inability to live up to what we ourselves

consider proper standards of right and wrong—is a special segment of this far more general experience of our inadequacy according to the standards which we have accepted as appropriate for ourselves. This does not mean that our standards are always realistic. It does mean that all of us often feel inadequate and guilty because what we see when we look at ourselves honestly we do not like.

Because the experience of failure is true and universal it is important to confront our feelings of guilt openly, and to seek the help of somebody who can interpret them to us in the light of our God-given destiny. It need not be a pastor to whom we speak honestly about ourselves, but there should be somebody to whom we can talk about the feelings which poison our relationships to God, to our fellowmen, and to ourselves.

We have learned that a person who has not come to terms with his guilt feelings may subconsciously punish himself by driving his car into a tree or slicing a finger while cutting the roast for dinner. It is far better to leave the judgment to God than to become our own executioners. Yet this is the tragedy of the life apart from God. People who cannot say, "He who judges me is the Lord," do consciously or unconsciously judge themselves and do it very badly, for they are too self-indulgent and too hard on themselves at the same time. We are much better off with God as our judge than with ourselves or our neighbors in this important position.

The Augsburg Confession makes one further observation: "It is not necessary to enumerate all trespasses and sins." People can become obsessed with their own failures. More interested in talking about themselves than doing something to serve God and their neighbor, they become paralyzed by their inadequacies and chew them over and over again as a cow chews her cud. "Don't bother," says the Augsburg Confession. Absolution can free you from yourself, from your obsession with your own failures and accomplishments. The purpose of confession and absolution is to free the Christian from himself for others. He is forgiven so that he may be able to forgive and serve.

Article XII. Repentance

It is sad but true that even the most meaningful moment in life fades away and loses some of its significance as the years pass. Human memory is short, and we forget easily. We change, and what was very important for us at one time loses all meaning when our values and standards have shifted. Thus we may think nostalgically of the wonderful moment when we first were allowed to drive the car, when we had our first date, when we graduated from school. There are many such moments in every life: the first real job, marriage, promotion, the birth of a child. All are very important and meaningful, yet nobody is able to preserve forever the fresh and enthusiastic attitude which gave these events their special excitement. Life tends to wear us down and curb our enthusiasm.

This seems equally true in our life with God and his people. All the great Christians of the past describe times of dryness, of boredom, of doubt, even of despair. This erosion of enthusiasm and commitment seems to happen gradually. Some people who at one period of their life found the relationship to God to be the source of all strength and comfort may become slowly sidetracked and drift away from the faith and the community which proclaims it. There is not a church anywhere which has not experienced this fading of leadership.

To be sure, other people take the place of those who leave, and somehow the church goes on—but what does it mean to a once-faithful servant of God that he now has another master? What does it mean to a man who once was traveling toward the city of God that he is now bogged down in cares about money, power, and status, facing into quite another direction than the kingdom of God which he was seeking once upon a time?

However sad and depressing such a situation may be, the Augsburg Confession asserts that it is far from hopeless: "It is taught among us that those who sin after Baptism receive forgiveness of sin whenever they come to repentance, and absolution should not be denied them by the church."

All that is necessary to reverse the process leading toward despair is to repent. "Properly speaking, true repentance is nothing else than to have contrition and sorrow, or terror, on account of sin, and yet at the same time to believe the Gospel and absolution . . . and this faith will comfort the heart and again set it at rest."

The possibility for repentance is always present. Some insurance companies proclaim that their help is as close as the nearest telephone; all you need is a dime to call them collect, and you will even get the dime back. In order to repent, though, you need neither a dime nor a telephone. All you need is the courage to look at yourself honestly. If you have had an automobile accident you have to face the fact that your car is a wreck, people have been hurt, you are in need of help. If you are not willing to face the fact that an accident has occurred and just walk away, leaving the scene, your insurance company cannot help you. Before they can come to your assistance, you must face the facts.

Repentance as the Augsburg Confession describes it is nothing but facing the facts of a life without God. It is a life without meaning absorbed in trivialities and pretensions— "the tale told by an idiot, full of sound and fury, signifying nothing." The sound and the fury may temporarily cover up the idiocy of such a life— but only temporarily. Then, if you are young, you may want to escape by way of marijuana or LSD, or if you are older, by way of alcohol, or if you are stupid, by way of busy work, keeping the house clean or the office help terrorized—and if you are desperate, by way of suicide. Sooner or later sorrow or terror get to all of us— and sometimes they come together.

The Augsburg Confession does not claim that we can escape these furies; it says that they can be overcome again and again if we believe in the Gospel. The good news is that God knows all about us. We do not have to pretend anything. He has forgiven us and loves us nevertheless. We do not even have to pretend faith. If we want to trust God ever so tentatively, if we say, "Lord I believe, help thou my unbelief," he will understand us better than we understand ourselves. The faith the Augsburg Confession talks about is not faith in the Augsburg Confession, but faith in God's steadfast love.

But our article does not stop here; it adds: "Amendment of life and the forsaking of sin should then follow, for these must be the fruits of repentance."

Does this make sense? If he sees that his life has meaning, the man who has terrorized his employees because the meaning of his life depended upon their reaction of fear can find a new starting place. The woman who has interfered in the life of her children and made them and herself miserable does not have to live that way anymore if she accepts God's meaning for her life. The teenager who feels unloved and hopes to find love in total sexual promiscuity, but instead experiences total meaninglessness, can accept herself as a person rather than an object if she accepts God's love. These new possibilities, though, are not the conditions of God's love; they are its results. Repentance is not a work through which we deserve God's love; it is the recognition that God has loved us while we were undeserving, and that he wants us to accept his love without regard for our self-evaluation.

This renewal of life through repentance is not something that just happens once; it must happen all the time. The Augsburg

Confession continues: "Rejected here are those who teach that persons who have once become godly cannot fall again. Condemned on the other hand are the Novatians who denied absolution to such as had sinned after Baptism." It is for this reason that Luther tells us in the Small Catechism: "The old Adam in us, together with all sins and evil lusts, should be drowned by daily sorrow and repentance and be put to death, and the new man should come forth daily and rise up, cleansed and righteous, to live forever in God's presence." This, indeed, is the meaning of repentance.

Article XIII. The Use of the Sacraments

Whenever a mother threatens a disobedient child by telling him that she will call the policeman to punish him, she undermines an attitude of cooperation between citizen and law-enforcement officer which is essential for an orderly society. By teaching the child that the police are his enemy she makes it very difficult for him to see in law-enforcement a positive and useful activity supporting him and all his friends. The policeman becomes the person who spoils his fun and is thus "the enemy."

It is possible by false teaching to make it difficult for anybody to gain an adequate understanding of any important human activity. In this manner many of us have been confused and made unable to overcome certain prejudices learned in early childhood. Sex is dirty; to study is sissy; to show emotion is feminine; these are prejudices which, if learned early, can poison our life for years to come. Some people never manage to shake off the influence of such attitudes.

The Augsburg Confession claims that our relationship with God can also be perverted by false teaching. This is nowhere clearer than in our understanding of the Sacraments. Our attitude here tends to reveal our attitude toward God. Sacraments are for many people human devices to please God; they are used to show God how faithful we are. Using them in this manner indicates how wrongly we understand our relationship to God. The Augsburg Confession says: "It is taught among us that the sacraments were instituted not only to be signs by which people might be identified outwardly as Christians, but that they are signs and testimonies of God's will toward us for the purpose of awakening and strengthening our faith. For this reason they require faith, and they are rightly used when they are received in faith and for the purpose of strengthening faith."

God uses the Sacraments to show us his steadfast love, but many people believe that the Sacraments are devices we can use to endear ourselves to God or demonstrate our worthiness to him. Millions of Americans who consider themselves Christians and would be so counted on any census have never been baptized. The number who never go to Holy Communion is even greater.

There are a number of reasons for this. Some people just do not care enough about God and his church to bother. Then their neglect of the Sacraments is a perfectly proper demonstration of their rejection of the Christian faith.

But there are many others who do not partake of the Sacraments because, like the man who was scared with the police as a boy and now rejects all law-enforcement, they were told as children that God was interested only in good people and therefore his Sacraments are not for them. They never have "enough faith" to present themselves for baptism, and they never feel good enough to go to Holy Communion.

Of course, faith is important, but the Sacraments are for people of weak faith. If they are "for the purpose of strengthening faith," as the Augsburg Confession says, then the faith of the recipient must need strengthening.

Baptism is a form of washing. Those who are clean do not need it, only those who are dirty. It is silly to claim I am not clean enough to be washed. Without washing you will hardly get any cleaner. Yet so many people who sincerely refuse baptism are afraid that they are not clean enough and that this washing is reserved for those who are better Christians than they are.

Similarly, Holy Communion is a form of feeding. Bread and wine were the most basic kinds of food available in Jesus' time. If anybody was invited as a guest by a friend, he would receive bread and wine. Now it is foolish to say, "I am too hungry to be fed. I will wait till I am less hungry and then I will come for your food." But this is precisely what the person says who tells the pastor that he cannot come to Holy Communion because he is not good enough. It is really like saying, "Sorry I have to turn down your dinner invitation. I am too hungry." If anybody said this to you, you would consider him out of his mind. Yet people say this all the time to God. There is not a congregation where there are not some who have refused for years to go to the Lord's table because they were too hungry.

There must be an explanation for this seemingly perverse attitude. The clue seems to be the last sentence in our article of the Augsburg Confession which states that the Sacraments "require faith, and they are rightly used when they are received in faith and for the purpose of strengthening faith."

Those Christians who are afraid of using the Sacraments have a false notion of faith. In Tillich's phrase they distort faith intellectually, emotionally, or voluntaristically. This means that some think they do not believe enough. They assume that the faith required is the acceptance of certain statements in the creed, and they may have difficulty accepting quite a few of them. Thus they consider themselves unready for the Sacrament because they do not believe a sufficient number of propositions.

Others again think that faith is an emotional response, a warm feeling that they may once have had, though it is now lost. In the absence of this warm feeling they feel unworthy of the Sacraments and wait for the return of the emotional fire before presenting themselves to the Lord.

Finally there are those who see in faith an act of the will. To have faith is for them to have their will under control, and not to be distracted in any manner by other cares of the world. Faith for them is to will one thing, and they are aware of the fact that they unfortunately want many things and are not in command of their will. Here the Sacrament is shunned because faith is considered too diffuse and not sufficiently single-minded to make us worthy of this great gift.

But faith is not intellectual assent to propositions or warmth or intensity of religious feeling, or even singleness of mind in the vision of God. Faith is simply to trust Christ. If you only trust him and say, "Lord, I believe, help thou my unbelief," he is yours and you are his, and you are ready for the use of the Sacraments.

Article XIV. Order in the Church

One of the most prevalent errors in our age is the notion that freedom and order are opposites. Many people believe that order is the mortal enemy of freedom, and that those who advocate freedom must of necessity oppose order of any kind.

A very simple illustration will show the foolishness of this analysis. If you want to drive from the town where you live to a nearby town, your freedom to take this trip and to arrive safely at your destination depends almost entirely on the order prevailing on the highway. Only because people have learned to drive on the right side of the road, to pass on the left, and to stop for red lights and stop signs do you have the freedom to get where you want to go. Order is not the enemy of your freedom to travel, it is its condition.

This is equally true in the family, in business, in government, and in the church. Only if a family operates according to some generally observed rules are the individual members free to eat and sleep, to work and play. A totally chaotic family would mean that the children starve, the father loses his job, and the mother her mind. You may have observed such families in operation, but they hardly strike you as examples of freedom.

61

A business enterprise, a store, a factory, or a farm depends for the freedom of employers and employees on order. The more orderly the operation the more freedom for all concerned; total disorder would in all cases mean bankruptcy, and that is hardly the basis for freedom in any meaningful sense.

Similarly, "government of law, not of men," the slogan of all sound government, is an appeal to order as the basis of freedom. Government by men rather than by laws means an emphasis on personalities and preferences, on tastes and prejudices, which has always produced chaos and never freedom.

It is therefore not surprising that the Augsburg Confession, in discussing the way the church should be administered, pleads for order. We read: "It is taught among us that nobody should publicly teach or administer the sacraments in the church without a regular call."

The church is as dependent for its freedom on order as are all other human institutions. This reminds us that the church is not only called into existence by God to serve mankind but also administered by men. It is a very human institution as well. But it is more difficult to bring order into the church than into a school or a business. The reasons are many, but three may deserve special mention here.

The most obvious enemy of order in the church is sentimentality. No business could tolerate an accountant who cannot keep his books straight very long merely because he is so sincere, but people in the church are often willing to put up with totally incompetent persons because they have one single qualification: sincerity. Nothing ruins a Sunday school faster than a sincere but incompetent superintendent "supported" by sincere but incompetent teachers.

The hours wasted every Sunday morning by sheer incompetence —not ill will—stagger the imagination. If people were trained as little for public school teaching and prepared as little for each hour as some Sunday school teachers, our public school system would collapse. Yet public school teachers have their children for five days a week to teach them something; church school teachers often have them for barely one hour a week. Yet some will meet them sincere but unprepared.

Sincerity does not play the organ well, it does not sing the anthem correctly, it does not preach the sermon. A sermon is a form of speech. If it is to do any good it has to be carefully prepared. It is very arrogant to get up before a couple of hundred busy people on a Sunday morning and waste their time with unprepared remarks on sundry subjects. Yet it does happen all too often and it is an offense against good order. Sincerity is no excuse.

And neither is false piety. The Augsburg Confession has made it very clear that all men are sinners. But because of a false sense of piety people assume that the usual safeguards against sin that protect us from each other in other institutions are out of place in the church. Employees are generally protected against employers too stingy to pay them a decent wage. For this purpose we have unions or professional organizations which safeguard the interests of plumbers and truck drivers, college professors and postal employees. Yet because of a false sense of piety pastors are not protected, and since all men are sinners, even members of a church council, pastors are by far the lowest paid of the professional people who have had seven or eight years of education beyond high school.

But this false sense of piety works the other way too. There is a minimum of professional supervision for the minister, and while he may literally work himself to death because there is so much work to do, he can also waste more time and do less without anybody really knowing it than any other employed person. A false piety which assumes that a minister is not really human encourages such a state of affairs.

Finally, there is plain ignorance which causes disorder in the church. We have become very efficient in our country. We know how to make almost everything efficiently, and we also know how to sell it. We do this at least as efficiently as any other country in the world.

Yet we are just plain ignorant when it comes to the work of the church. The average town of 30,000 people may have 20 churches with 20 different buildings all used at most 20 hours out of the 168 per week. A disproportionate amount of resources is spent on such inefficiently utilized buildings. Thus they become millstones around the necks of the people who inherited them from previous generations and make it almost impossible for them to do their real work adequately today.

Teaching, preaching, and the administration of the Sacraments can become subordinated to building maintenance. The result may be ecclesiastical chaos. But there is little that can be done about it, for the two-party system which has served us so well in our country is unknown to the church. Out of a combination of sentimentality, false piety, and ignorance the fact of power and the control of power as a problem in the church is ignored. Since the churches favor government by men rather than by law, opposition to policies on both the local and the national level is always taken to be opposition to persons. The result is that there are no clearly marked channels for constructive criticism.

So if you don't like the church, you just pick up your marbles and go home. The land teems with ex-church-members who left not because of any great theological difficulty but because there was no way for them to express opposition except by leaving altogether.

The Augsburg Confession advocates order in the church. Having no elector or prince to help us out, as Luther did, we might have to come up with some new answers. There is no time to waste.

Article XV. Church Usages

It is easier to split a church by removing the stained-glass windows from the building—be they ever so ugly—than by removing the Gospel from the preaching. This statement may sound exaggerated, but look around you and see if it isn't true. What divides churches? People apparently are willing to put up with some pretty weird preaching without becoming too upset. They tolerate ignorance of the Word of God and hostility to the faith of the church, but they feel very strongly about the sacred equipment. There are churches where every reminder of the ancient faith has been removed—but they still use pews and lecterns, the order of service, and hymns. One gains the impression that the common attitude is: change the faith, if you must, but do not change the liturgy, do not change the hymn tunes (you may change the words), and above all, do not change the chancel furniture, including the painting above the altar.

The Augsburg Confession tries to put these questions into perspective. "With regard to church usages that have been established by men, it is taught among us that those usages are to be observed which may be observed without sin and which contribute to peace and good order in the church."

The customs of the church have all been established by men.

There are no God-given liturgical rubrics or directives for church architecture. None of the hymns we sing are in the Bible, and the Holy Spirit did not compose "The Old Rugged Cross."

But we must go a step farther. None of the activities of the church, in the form in which we now engage in them, are divinely appointed. Neither service at 11 A.M. nor Sunday school, neither world missions nor college education, absolutely none of the activities of the church as now practiced are sacrosanct. These forms have all been established by men over a period of almost 2000 years. Of themselves they are neither right nor wrong; the only valid way to judge them is to see whether or not they support the people of God in their march into the future and in their task of proclaiming the Gospel in word and deed in this world.

Unlike some other Christians who wanted to reestablish the usages of the first century in the 16th, the signers of the Augsburg Confession were willing to accept many of the customs that had developed during the centuries because they were useful to the Gospel. They sang the old hymns and wrote many new ones; they did not go back merely to chanting the Psalms of the Old Testament as if these were the only appropriate songs of the church. They did not destroy the statues and images in the church as long as they were able to make sure that people would not worship them. They realized that many of these outward forms and customs helped people to understand the Gospel better. People can learn a lot of theology by using the liturgy, singing hymns, or even looking at pictures and statues. We do not learn only by listening, we learn also by doing and seeing.

But the Augsburg Confession makes the essential condition for retaining ancient forms or introducing new ones very clear: "We accompany these observances with instruction so that consciences may not be burdened by the notion that such things are necessary for salvation."

Whenever old or new customs create tension in a congregation today, the reason is invariably that there has been too little instruction. The old was removed and the new introduced without explaining the reasons behind the changes, so that people became confused and resentful. Most people are actually willing to accept a great deal of change in our rapidly changing world if they are allowed to share the reasons for the changes. Instruction must accompany all observances, be they old or new.

Yet in the church we do so many things which have become merely routine, and we never ask ourselves why we are doing them one way and not another. There may be good reasons for our customs, but unless we are willing to explain the meaning of our observances, religious ritual degenerates into mumbo-jumbo which confuses and mystifies rather than educates and edifies. This is true for "low-church" as well as "high-church" practices. For the uninitiated outsider a low-church prayer meeting may be as bewildering as a high-church Eucharist, but both may be meaningful if people "accompany these observances with instruction."

Despite this obvious need, in most of our churches there is very little instruction about the shape of our form of worship available to the visitor who comes to worship with us. We assume that he will understand what we are doing. This assumption is particularly unjustified in that many of us don't really understand ourselves what we are doing. The Augsburg Confession demands regular instruction.

This article has still another implication. It demands frequent reassessment of what we are doing. All the present usages in the church have been established by men. As we observed earlier, this is as true of our educational system and of our home and foreign mission program as it is of the organization of our local congregation and of our Sunday worship. The question must be asked continually: Do these patterns contribute to the "proclamation of the Gospel and the teaching about faith in Christ" or are they ways of "propitiating God and earning grace"? This question must be asked in every generation, since what was once a useful instrument of the Gospel may become in time merely a pious routine.

We must have the courage to change, not in order to be up to date, but to serve the Gospel. Not all changes are functional. Not everything new serves God better than the old. Monastic vows and tradition concerning distinction of food—rejected by the Augsburg Confession—were once the very latest thing, the wave of the future. But since they were understood to "earn grace and make satisfaction for sin," the Augsburg Confession considered them "useless and contrary to the Gospel."

What are the practices today which are designed "to earn grace and make satisfaction for sin"? Look around you. Have we not developed our own ways of propitiating God and earning grace? Is it waving the American flag? Is it marching around the Post Office with placards? Is it the "New Morality" or defending the Old Morality? Is it Anti-Communism or Internationalism? From reading some of the letters to the editor one gains the distinct impression that we have our own "ordinances and traditions through which we are going to propitiate God and earn grace." To us Article XV of the Augsburg Confession says today: "Traditions . . . by which it is intended to earn grace and make satisfaction for sin are useless and contrary to the Gospel."

Article XVI. Civil Government

Those who have considered the Augsburg Confession old-fashioned and irrelevant will discover that in Article XVI it is as contemporary as the daily newspaper.

On the surface this article defends the hallowed tradition of evangelical Christians that to serve God means participating openly and actively in the affairs of the world: "It is taught among us that all government in the world and all established rule and laws were instituted and ordained by God for the sake of good order, and that Christians may without sin occupy civil offices or serve as princes and judges, render decisions and pass sentence according to imperial and other existing laws, punish evildoers with the sword, engage in just wars, serve as soldiers, buy and sell, take required oaths, possess property, be married, etc."

The argument is clearly directed against two fronts. On the one hand, it opposes the perfectionism of the Anabaptists, who withdrew into the wilderness and created their own isolated communities to avoid sin. On the other hand, it rejects the stance of the monk who abandons participation in the secular world and hopes to please God with his vows of obedience, chastity, and poverty.

Responsible Christian life means participation in all the difficult and controversial areas of human existence. It means to be present where the power is, where the decisions are being made. The Confession mentions specifically close contact with political, military, and economic power. Christians are called to intelligent and responsible citizenship. They are warned not to abandon the power structure but rather to infiltrate it. Verbal criticism, may it be ever so eloquent, is not enough. The Augsburg Confession considers withdrawal from the fray a false kind of enthusiasm. It speaks to our time and to all those disenchanted people young and old who, appalled by the complexities of life, the ambiguity of power, and the reality of evil, believe that the morally responsible action is to "drop out."

In direct opposition to such counsel, the advice of the Augsburg Confession is "get with it." Study where your influence can make a difference so that "each according to his own calling, manifest Christian love and genuine good works in his station of life."

The Confession emphasizes the importance of knowing where each, "according to his own calling," can do the most good. It is a part of the responsibility of every Christian to ask himself, "Where can I, with the abilities and the education I have received or may still receive, make my influence felt?" Do not play the grandstand to get attention; get involved where it counts, even if it does not make the headlines.

In very specific terms, it is doubtful whether people will change the world very drastically by ignoring the political and economic structures which determine change. Piety is not enough. Ignorance of the way change is brought about is irresponsibility and even sin. If you do not know who runs your company and your union, your city, your state, and your country, if you have not learned how to influence those people by personal contacts or letters and through concerted action, then you are really not "manifesting Christian love and genuine good works in your station of life" even though you may have a perfect attendance record in Sunday school and be able to rattle off the names of all the books of the Bible.

Your station in life happens to be, among other things, that of a citizen of the most powerful democracy in the world. This is a heavy responsibility, and you cannot escape it. You follow your calling by the way you vote for city council, for school board, for Congress, and for the President of the United States.

In the same way, your vote in your labor union election or the advice you give in your company is part of your calling, and so is the way you spend or invest your money. All this is covered by Article XVI when it speaks of "buying and selling, taking required oaths, and possessing property" as appropriate to the Christian.

Because we are citizens of a democracy and live in a rapidly changing world, all of our social responsibilities have developed implications which Melanchthon and the signers of the Augsburg Confession could not even have imagined—but for us these implications are clear. There is a direct line from taking the required oaths to voting, and from buying and selling to the stock market. And since government exists for the sake of good order, concern with national and international conflicts and with efforts to reduce disorder are Christian duties.

There is one notion in Article XVI which is particularly interesting and controversial in our time. We read that Christians may "engage in just wars." This notion opens a most acutely debated issue, namely the question of selective conscientious objection to military service.

The very concept of a just war, as set forth in the Augsburg Confession, implies the possibility of an unjust war, and the insistence that Christians may participate without sin in just wars clearly implies that they may not do so in unjust wars. This is a most important distinction for our time. If the Augsburg Confession is right that a distinction can and must be made between just and unjust wars, then the only question is, "What are the criteria for such a distinction?" Once such criteria have been established it becomes most dangerous for me to participate in what I consider an unjust war. Thus, our article concludes, "Accordingly Christians are obliged to be subject to civil authority and obey its commands and laws *in all that can be done without sin* [italics added]. But when commands of the civil authority cannot be obeyed without sin, we must obey God rather than men (Acts 5:29)."

Regardless of the merits of the arguments in a particular situation, those who take the Augsburg Confession seriously, and even more significantly, those who take the Bible seriously, must defend the right of people to selective conscientious objection to war. If a person believes that a particular war in which his country is engaged is unjust, he should be classified as a conscientious objector. Indeed, while the Augsburg Confession seems to condemn the pacifist, the objector to all war, it does give support to the selective conscientious objector, to the person who objects to a particular war as unjust.

The only cogent argument against this interpretation of the Augsburg Confession would be the claim that since Hiroshima the entire concept of the "just war" has become obsolete. A good case can be made for the assertion that no war which would result in the extinction of the human race could ever be just. What has happened is that the very character of war has so radically changed that notions borrowed from the 16th century are simply not applicable in the atomic age. But if one reasons in this manner, it might demand a radical pacifist position from all Christians, as indeed some theologians claim. It would deny the right to selective conscientious objection only because participation in any war would be completely indefensible. Thus it appears that selective conscientious objection to war is the most positive position toward war a Christian can possibly defend. To say, "right or wrong my country," is clearly against Article XVI of the Augsburg Confession, and what is more important, it is clearly against the First Commandment, which says, "I am the Lord, thy God. Thou shalt have no other gods before me"—not even the state.

Article XVII. The Return of Christ to Judgment

The most significant difference between the 20th century and all earlier ages of human history is not the vast change in technology; it is a basic difference in mood.

The technological changes which this century has brought, of course, are incredible in their scope. In all of human history from the beginning of man to the year 1900 the speed with which man could travel changed less than in the few years since that time. The entire development of power at the disposal of man in the thousands of years of human history up to 1900 is dwarfed by the development in the last few decades. Similar assertions could be made about other technological achievements—last but not least our incredible ability to kill and destroy. Yet the most basic change in our day is a change in mood rather than in power, in our attitude toward life rather than in the way we actually live.

People are deceived by the apparent similarity of our food, shelter, and clothing to those of previous generations into thinking that not much has really happened. We eat the same types of food as our ancestors did a thousand years ago; it may be inefficient to obtain our protein by running food through an animal—supporting this animal until we can obtain the steaks and chops we want. There may be more direct ways of securing the necessary nourishment for man than such old-fashioned patterns—but so far we have been unwilling to change. Similarly, a house built in colonial style may be a little out of place in urban America, but it gives people a cozy feeling, so that they are willing to live with the anachronism. Our clothing is basically similar to that of previous generations—except when we want to travel into outer space. The buttons on the sleeves of men's coats designed to keep English soldiers from wiping their noses on their sleeves have been kept by 20th century Americans out of respect for the past.

All these comforting "remembrances of things past," however, are really quite unimportant. Our mood, our basic attitude toward life, has changed. Our ancestors believed that the world was not subject to human control, that whatever men might do, their physical environment and they themselves would not substantially change. We are convinced today that for good or ill we have the power to change our environment, ourselves, and the shape of future generations.

The philosophies of the past were essentially programs supposed to teach us how to cope with life. The basic character of life would not change. The wise man learned to live with its many vicissitudes. Man had to adjust to his environment, and religion was one of the aids in this process.

The tremendous difference in the modern mood is the underlying conviction that man can basically change his environment and perhaps even himself. Some contemporaries conclude from this fact that religion is no longer necessary. Others again insist that for this very reason it is more necessary than ever in order to supply some guidelines for the changes now possible.

It is quite apparent that such changes as man is able to bring about are not necessarily for the better. The new age of man was inauspiciously ushered in by the mass murder of tens of thousands of defenseless men, women, and children at Hiroshima. Since then the human world has teetered on the edge of the abyss of total destruction. The vision of the end of the world in flames is no longer limited to the last chapters in books on dogmatics; it is a human possibility contemplated seriously and with the help of the most sophisticated computers by the experts on "overkill" in Washington and Moscow and now also in Peking.

The ambiguity of this situation is illustrated by the literature of our time dealing with the future. The fact that man can change his environment and control or even change others now is taken for granted in all these books, but that such changes will be in man's interest is considered highly questionable. Most of the books dealing with man's future describe it in somber if not terrifying pictures. To the writers of our age the future looks so menacing precisely because man has so much power to influence it; it is man who represents the greatest danger to man. The increase of human power has been accompanied by the fear for his survival as a human being. That seems to be the message of the more sophisticated science fiction. Not the super-man but the inferior-man stares at us from the pages of these books. Big Brother is watching you!

But what has all this to do with Article XVII of the Augsburg Confession which states, "It is also taught among us that our Lord Jesus Christ will return on the last day for judgment"? In an age justly fearful of the apparently unlimited powers of man to destroy his world and himself, the Augsburg Confession proclaims that the symbol which dominates the final scene of human history is not the cloud but the cross.

The Christian proclamation in our time is a message of hope rather than despair because Christians believe that history is moving toward Jesus Christ. He is the "Alpha and Omega, who is and who is to come, the sovereign Lord of all" (Rev. 1:8).

This conviction, expressed so clearly in Article XVII of the Augsburg Confession, makes the document relevant to people who have reason to fear that the end of history will be fire, radiation, and death.

If our analysis of the mood of the times is correct, most modern men believe the following to be true: not only do we have the power to change man and his world, we are also in the process of doing it right now, with ever increasing momentum. The frightful fact is that we are operating without any clear knowledge of what this is all about. We have the power to make these changes, but we have no clear idea how to use it. We want to create a new man in a new world, but we have no acceptable pattern for either.

In this crucial moment the church as an institution is preoccupied with backward-looking and navel-gazing. Those who are looking into the past are making the church into a museum displaying the faith of men of other times confronted by other problems than those we have described so far.

The Christian faith had one function when the central human problem was to cope with a harsh and unyielding universe. Now that this universe has become pliable and apparently far too responsive to man for his own good, this same faith has another function as well. It has to direct our power to change the world and thus bring order out of our anarchy.

The task to which the Augsburg Confession calls us in our time is to proclaim Christ to the world as the man who came that we might live and who is still coming toward us that we may live more abundantly. The future is his also.

Article XVIII. Freedom of the Will

When our ancestors made their way first to America and then westward across the country, expanding the frontiers of the new world, it was easier to believe in freedom of the will than it is today. Personal decisions that seemed to be clearly the result of individual choices had apparently motivated these people, so that freedom of the will became part of the common faith of America. More people here than anywhere else in the world believed firmly that man makes himself, that he can be in fact a self-made man.

It is therefore hard for us to realize that the high opinion of man's ability to shape his life so prevalent in this country is a minority view among the world's people. The overwhelming majority are convinced that forces over which we have little or no control determine our destiny.

There are those who believe in the stars. They look anxiously into the newspaper or into their special astrological magazines to see what their horoscope has in store for them. Their decisions and choices do not determine their fate, but only the combination of the stars and planets on a particular day.

Millions of people all over the world are convinced that some

Karma or Kismet determines their life, that they are merely actors who act out parts in a play they have not written and whose end they neither know nor can affect in any way. Death does not necessarily end the play but may end only one act. The belief in reincarnation suggests that such a play may have innumerable acts, all equally beyond the control of the actors.

While these beliefs may seem fairly alien to most Americans we accept versions of determinism which amount to the same basic denial of freedom of the will. Advocates of white power and black power proclaim with equal stridency that we are determined to be what we are by the pigmentation of the skin with which we happen to be born. Depending on the speaker we are told that white people or black people are basically good and will be the salvation of the world, and conversely that black people or white people are basically evil and threaten the world with destruction. These views are more or less eloquently presented in every city of this country, and millions believe the spokesmen of this kind of racial determinism who make man's destiny the result of the color of his skin. Besides the white and black racists there are the psychological and genetic determinists who claim that it is our environment or our genetic structure which determines our fate. There is little we can do to escape the pigeonholes they have prepared for us and to which they assign us with the help of their tests and measurements.

Lately even some theologians have joined the general chorus of those who say that the future is assured. With an optimism quite alien to the biblical witness and to Christian tradition they promise us that the future is secure regardless of our actions. Whatever survives deserves to survive and life and history as well as God and the church are always with the winner. The determinism of Social Darwinism has learned to speak in theological language and tells us confidently that just because God is no longer in his heaven all is right with the world. Whatever happens is good because the "good" is that which happens.

This is the much advertised theology of the "world come of age" and the "secular city." In the midst of war its spokesmen cry, "peace, peace"—and there is no peace. In the midst of hate they cry "love, love"—and there is no love. In the midst of the decay and death caused by the pollution of the sea, the air, the land, and the minds of men they cry, "life, life"—and there is no life. Convinced that the world is getting constantly better they offer us no evidence but their own dogmas.

Against all these progress- and evolution-intoxicated theologians of glory the Augsburg Confession asserts soberly: "It is also taught among us that man possesses some measure of freedom of the will which enables him to live an outwardly honorable life and to make choices among the things that reason comprehends."

The Augsburg Confession does not question that man can function more or less successfully in this world if he uses his reason. He has "some measure of freedom," and thus he can organize his life, his community, his country, perhaps even the world, if he puts his reason to work. Our confession allows for more freedom for good or ill than the advocates of fate and determinism would like to grant us. We have the limited power to make our life better as well as worse. Any absolute determinism is rejected.

But when it comes to man's relationship to God, the Augsburg Confession denies man the capacity to achieve anything apart from God's grace: "Without the grace, help, and activity of the Holy Spirit man is not capable of making himself acceptable to God, of fearing God and believing in God with his whole heart, or expelling inborn evil lusts from his heart. This is accomplished by the Holy Spirit, who is given through the Word of God."

It is apparent that in its discussion of the freedom of the will the Augsburg Confession is not concerned with psychology or philosophy. It is interested only in man's relationship to God. Against all those who made this bond a simple human possibility our confession asserts that only God can establish as well as maintain such a relationship. When some contemporary theologians claim that they no longer believe in God they are saying nothing new, but merely restating the very old and sad truth here so clearly expressed, that "man is not capable of fearing God and believing in God." It was always thus. But to Christians it is hardly a reason for bragging and thumping one's chest. No reasonable man boasts about a fatal disease—why should men pride themselves that they suffer from unbelief, "the sickness unto death"?

At the same time our confession makes it very clear that those of us who believe also have nothing to boast about. Faith is the gift of the Holy Spirit. Because we are unable to fear and trust God with our own power, we cannot take any credit for our faith. We must say with the Apostle Paul, "He that glories, let him glory in the Lord" (2 Cor. 10:17).

Article XIX. The Cause of Sin

Even the most superficial readers of newspaper headlines would have to admit that we live in a troubled world. From the personal problems of sickness and boredom to the international tensions which result in armed conflict among nations we are everywhere confronted by questions to which we have no real answers.

Of course, a variety of answers have been suggested, but all seem pitifully inadequate. There are the faddists who tell us that health can be assured by means of certain odd "natural" foods or peculiar exercises. All problems, they suggest, could be solved if we were to adopt their particular diet. Some feel so strongly about this that they claim that the obvious defects in our society are the result of the chemicals introduced into our food and our water. They assert that not only our personal health but even our national security is threatened by the use of such chemicals.

While there may very well be some truth in the charges that insecticides and weed-killers are dangerous, it is hard to believe that our use of certain chemicals is the source of all evil, especially since it is apparent that evil was quite prevalent long before the invention of these modern devices.

Others tell us with equal sincerity that evil could be abolished if we would only change our economic system from one based on competition and the profit motive as basic incentives to one which would let the state be the universal employer and class loyalty the basic motive for work. Here again the solution looks unimpressive in view of the admitted existence of all kinds of evil in countries which have adopted such economic systems. Whatever else happened in China after 1945, evil did not disappear; otherwise the Red Guards would not have all this trouble uprooting it.

Still others claim that if only black men would rule, evil would fade away, since in the view of these prophets evil is directly related to "whiteness." Apparently good is an aspect of skin pigmentation; the darker the skin, the better the man. This theory also lacks power to persuade in view of the way in which black people in power kill each other in certain parts of Africa, quite in line with the patterns established by those people we call "white." Pigmentation is an aspect of our skin, not the seat of our conscience.

The list of phony solutions to the obvious predicament of man is endless , but as soon as they are described most people recognize their inadequacy. Evil is undeniably real, but the cause of evil eludes us.

It is the assertion of the Augsburg Confession that the cause of sin is the perverted human will. This is how it is stated: "It is taught among us that although almighty God has created and still preserves nature, yet sin is caused in all wicked men and despisers of God by the perverted will . . . . as soon as God withdraws his support, the will turns away from God to evil."

There are some young people who consider themselves very radical, who claim, "You cannot trust anybody over thirty." The Augsburg Confession is far more radical. It says, "You cannot trust any man." The people over thirty are not trustworthy—and neither are the people under thirty. According to the Augsburg Confession these young radicals are just plain sentimentalists.

The root of the trouble is not outside of men at all. It is not the economy or the political situation, the baseness of other races, the ingratitude of youth, or the insensitivity of the old. The problem lies with every man. White men are untrustworthy because they are sinful, not because they are white; the same goes for black men.

It is men who make capitalism and communism work badly, to the disadvantage of other men. According to the Augsburg Confession the problem of man is man. Any solution which evades this fact must of necessity fail.

But what is it that perverts the human will and makes it an instrument of evil? There are a number of very obvious causes. All men are unreasonably selfish; they prefer their own lesser good to the greater good of others. This makes them litter streets, evade income tax, break up homes, and do all sorts of obviously evil things. The boy who steps on the newly poured cement sidewalk in order to perpetuate his footprints expresses the same selfishness that makes his father repeat false rumors about a colleague started by the man who wants his job. The truck driver who endangers the life of everybody on the road by using pep-pills displays the same kind of basic selfishness that motivates the pretty young thing to make eyes at the married man in her office.

Men are full of unreasonable pride. The desire to feel superior poisons the relationship of the sexes, of generations, of races, and of nations. Men think they are superior to women. Every race considers itself better than other races, and every nation and tribe believes that it is by far the best. It is out of such foolish pride that the tensions between men are born and their relationship to each other perverted.

Men are full of idolatry. They worship false gods. Power, money, fame, pleasure are some idols that make men's life together almost impossible. Look at a disastrous conflict on any level and it will not be hard to discover some idolatry as the cause of the evil. The difference between conflicts in the family and among the nations is quantitatively vast, but qualitatively these conflicts are amazingly similar. In all cases they result from the perverted will. One of the insights of the Augsburg Confession is that it is not in the intellect but in the will of man that the root of the problem of evil is to be found. Evil starts in the heart of man, and in the heart of man it must, therefore, be overcome.

Article XX. Faith and Good Works

The attentive reader of these comments, if there is such a person, must have noticed by now that the central assertion of the Augsburg Confession is: Man is acceptable to God because God has accepted him and not because of anything man has done. While this state of affairs may at first seem quite surprising, there are experiences in life so similar that they help us to understand this phenomenon better. It happens in everyday life that a girl may become lovely by being loved. She may seem unattractive and awkward, a veritable ugly duckling, until somebody takes a real interest in her, gives her a lot of attention, and loves her. As she becomes aware of this new situation, which has been created by the fact that she is loved, her entire personality may change. She may actually become what she has been so far only in the eyes of this one man who saw something that nobody else could see. The "ugly duckling" may change into a swan. This change can be so real that after a while it is noticed by everybody.

This phenomenon occurs often; it can be frequently observed because most sensitive young people in our culture seem to pass through moments of severe and genuine self-rejection. They actually hate themselves and periodically see nothing attractive in themselves at all. They feel not only that nobody loves them but also that they are not at all lovable; therefore they view any love shown to them with profound suspicion.

Yet, when they have finally become convinced that they are truly loved, not as objects but as persons, they often change into more generous, open, and warmer human beings.

The Augsburg Confession claims that the human situation in relation to God is somewhat analogous. We are not really able to live "good" lives until we have accepted the fact that God loves us even though we are unworthy of his love. God does not love us because we live good lives but because he loves us, and because we have become aware of this love and gratefully accept it we are in turn able to live lives of love. Thus good works follow faith, which is the realization of our acceptance by God. They are not the reason or condition for this acceptance.

The trouble with the approach to God by means of good works, against which the Augsburg Confession argues, is that it prevents these works from really being good. Our Confession claims that if you do certain deeds in order to score points with God you have to ask yourself, "What actions receive the highest score?" rather than, "What action is really of help to my neighbor?" As a result, all such "good works" become selfish and evil.

This can be illustrated by the various attitudes toward begging in different religious traditions. Giving alms to beggars has been considered a "good work" in almost all major religions. It was the case among the Christians in Luther's time. People believed that by giving alms they could acquire merits before God. Thus persons who asked for alms and depended on them were necessary. As a result beggars performed a useful function for the community by making alms-giving possible. Indeed, it was considered the special mark of distinction of certain religious organizations that they supported themselves largely by begging. This produced merits in two ways: The person begging achieved merits by demonstrating his admirable humility, and the person giving alms acquired merits by demonstrating his equally admirable charity.

If one were to abolish the need for begging by finding useful work for the unemployed, adequate homes for orphans, special care and rehabilitation for the blind, the crippled, and all other handicapped people, one would threaten the whole merit system, which needed both beggars and givers in order to furnish opportunities to perform meritorious "good works." Thus, because it was oriented toward the performance of meritorious works rather than the solution of problems of human need, the system of "good works" actually interfered with the most constructive solution to the human problem of poverty and begging.

For this reason the Augsburg Confession can say in our article: "In former times . . . for the most part sermons were concerned with childish and useless works like rosaries, the cult of saints, monasticism, pilgrimages, appointed fasts, holy days, brotherhoods, etc." All these "good works" seemed good only if the purpose of life was the achievement of merits. If, however, the purpose of the Christian life was the kind of service which would actually aid the neighbor to live a more human life, then all these so-called "good works" appeared "childish and useless." Merits are simply irrelevant if the purpose of the Christian life is to do whatever will support other human beings in their search for meaning and fulfillment.

Justification by faith did not interfere with good works, according to the Augsburg Confession; rather, it alone made them possible. It changed the basic motivation of man from the self-seeking profit motive obsessed with the accumulation of merits to a service motive concerned with the true welfare of the fellow man. Now, instead of supporting beggars by alms, the causes that made people into beggars could be abolished; people who had been forced to beg in order to survive were enabled to support themselves or be supported in a manner less destructive to their human dignity. Thus our article concludes: "It is also taught among us that good works should and must be done, not that we are to rely on them to earn grace but that we may do God's will and glorify him." We do God's will and glorify him when we accept his love without questioning and quibbling and share it with a world which needs such open, accepting, and reconciling love more than anything else. "Consequently this teaching concerning faith is not to be accused of forbidding good works but is rather to be praised for teaching that good works are to be done and for offering help as to how they may be done."

Article XXI. The Cult of Saints

The most effective teaching is done by example. Patterns of behavior, especially, are taught most adequately by demonstration rather than exhortation. Ask yourself, "Where did I learn my basic outlook on life?" The answer is, "In some life situation." Probably you learned your basic style of life in your family, from living with your parents and your brothers and sisters.

When there is no family to teach us these patterns of behavior other communities take its place. The peer group, the people of similar age with whom we live, often become the source of standards for our behavior. We learn by observing them and imitating their attitudes toward life.

The important thing to remember is that verbal exhortation by itself is most ineffective. The mother who tells her children not to lie but solves every crisis in her family by making promises to the children she has no intention of keeping teaches her children to lie, despite all her words against lying. It is the demonstration which counts, not the exhortation. The father who talks a great deal about safe driving to his son but takes chances whenever he finds he can get away with it, or drives within the speed limit only when a police car is around, might as well forget the good advice. The boy will follow his example, not his words.

This, by the way, is one of the problems with Sunday school. Most Sunday schools have as one of their objectives to teach people what is right and what is wrong in the light of the Christian Gospel. Now, you can teach people in Sunday school that David came after Saul and that there are four Gospels and the Gospel according to John has a different approach from those of the other three. But that has nothing to do with right and wrong. To teach patterns of behavior you have to *do* something, not only talk. Unfortunately, what we do in Sunday school and what we talk about are frequently diametrically opposed to each other. We talk about love to the neighbor while little David kicks little Susie under the table. We talk about cooperation while demonstrating utter failure to cooperate. We talk about dedicating our entire lives to Christ while the teacher demonstrates that he was unwilling to dedicate a couple of hours on Saturday to prepare himself adequately for the presentation of his lesson. The frequently observed failure of Sunday school is the result of our inability to make exhortation and demonstration work together. Children learn from the demonstration. They have learned to disregard mere exhortations long ago and call them "phony."

In fact one of the major reasons for the present conflict between generations so flagrantly illustrated in the "hippie" movement is the inability of young people to see any similarity between what adults say is right and wrong and what they actually do. This affects their attitude toward the President of the United States as well as toward their teachers and parents. The church is particularly subject to this criticism because it seems to talk so very much and do so very little. Its words and deeds seem ridiculously incongruous.

Now, what has all this to do with Article XXI of the Augsburg Confession? "It is also taught among us that saints should be kept in remembrance so that our faith may be strengthened when we see what grace they received and how they were sustained by faith."

The Augsburg Confession declares that we learn by example, and that those who have set an example in the past as well as those who are doing so now are very helpful in guiding us into the Christian life. The Confession continues, "Moreover, their good works are to be an example for us, each of us in his own calling."

We all need models to help us share our lives. The so-called "saints" are helpful because they show us how other people have faced problems similar to ours in similar situations. The example which the Augsburg Confession uses is King David. It says that he should serve as an example for the German emperor. The interesting thing about David is that he was everything but a "saint" in the ordinary sense of this word. In ordinary language a saint is a person who does nothing wrong, who is perfect. You don't have to be an expert Bible scholar to know that David was no such saint. He had problems with everybody, and many of them were his own fault. He had difficulties with his boss (Saul), mistreated his employees (Uriah), had a terrible record with women (Bathsheba), and managed to raise his son as a first-class juvenile delinquent (Absalom). Nevertheless, he was a saint, according to the Augsburg Confession, simply because he was a sinner who depended entirely on God's grace and was sustained in all the vicissitudes of his life, many of them of his own making, by his faith in God's power and love. David helps us, not because he was so perfect but because he was so obviously imperfect. Since God was willing to show his steadfast love to David, we have every reason to hope that he will show his steadfast love to us as well. The story of David does not merely tell us that God is love; it shows us what God's love means in the case of an extraordinarily gifted, complicated, disobedient, and selfish man who in spite of all his shortcomings trusted God and was saved.

The Augsburg Confession makes it very clear that saints cannot help us. "It cannot be proved from the Scriptures that we are to invoke saints or seek help from them. 'For there is one mediator between God and men, Christ Jesus' (I Tim. 2:5)." But saints can serve as examples of God's power and of his willingness to use weak and sinful human beings to accomplish his purposes. The saints demonstrate in their lives that God can use people like us to build his kingdom.

Peter is a greater saint because he denied Jesus three times than he would have been had he been more courageous. Those who have gone through similar experiences are reassured by this odd saint to trust God's grace rather than their own courage. This is what makes Thomas such a comfort to us, *because* he doubted the resurrection, not in spite of it. We can learn from him how God's grace can overcome our unbelief and doubt. The true saints of God are not moral supermen but justified sinners. They show us that God saves by demonstration, not exhortation.

"Divine folly is wiser than the wisdom of man, and divine weakness stronger than man's strength. My brothers, think what sort of people you are whom God has called. Few of you are men of wisdom, by any human standard; few are powerful or highly born. Yet, to shame the wise, God has chosen what the world counts folly, and to shame what is strong, God has chosen what the world counts weakness.

"He has chosen things low and contemptible, mere nothings, to overthrow the existing order. And so there is no place for human pride in the presence of God" (1 Cor. 1:25-29, NEB).

Article XXIII. The Marriage of Priests

The 22nd to 28th articles of the Augsburg Confession deal with some of the major problems that faced the church in the 16th century. The writers of the Augsburg Confession were trying to win the support of the power structure—in this case Emperor Charles V —to bring about some basic changes in certain religious practices which were giving offense to many sincere Christians.

Today there is little disagreement that many of these criticisms were justified at the time. While little is gained by warming over old controversies, some of the issues raised in the "Articles about Matters in Dispute" are still of interest in our time. I shall here deal with those which seem to confront us with the most important issues.

Article XXIII of the Augsburg Confession discusses the Marriage of Priests. Pointing out that the law forbidding priests to marry is a relatively late requirement not based on the Scriptures but on later ecclesiastical authority, the subscribers of the Augsburg Confession want it abolished. While this may still be a live issue among Roman Catholic Christians in our time, it is obvious that Protestants settled this issue a long time ago. Nobody seriously advocates a law against married clergy, and even voluntary celibacy is often viewed with suspicion among Protestants.

Yet this article does raise the much debated issue of laws governing sexual behavior. There is hardly a more controversial topic today than this matter of the new sexual attitudes among Americans. Even if people claim that actual behavior has not changed as drastically as the news reports sometimes seem to indicate, it is certainly true that attitudes have changed and are still changing. People may not have behaved much differently in the so-called Victorian Age, but the public and official attitude toward sex was vastly different.

What does the Augsburg Confession have to say on this subject? It openly admits that sex is very important to most human beings and that any law which attempts to control or restrict sex is going to come under severe attack. The 16th century was not an age of great moral virtue; the emperor to whom the Augsburg Confession was presented had illegitimate children all over Europe. The bigamy of Philip of Hesse, one of the most eloquent and sincere supporters of the Reformation, was soon to become a public scandal. Nevertheless, at that time only the advisability of the law of celibacy for the clergy was openly questioned.

In contrast we see in our time that the whole structure of the relationship of the sexes as developed in the last 1900 years is being called into question. What is the reason for this great upheaval? There are two very obvious causes: our technological achievements and the pluralistic world in which we live. Medical technology has broken the ancient bonds between sex and reproduction as well as sexual restraint and physical health. We must have other reasons than fear of pregnancy or venereal disease to affirm sexual restraint. The pluralistic world means that everybody is made aware by the mass media of the widespread disagreement about sexual rules among intelligent and decent people, including justices of the Supreme Court and governors of states, bishops and famous theologians. We are no longer simply "tradition-directed," accepting the rules of the past as automatically binding; we want to be given reasons for the regulations we are supposed to follow.

Thus it is interesting that the Augsburg Confession actually approaches the subject of celibacy in a most reasonable manner. "Are the rules governing the behavior of priests making people better or worse?" It suggests that if they are making people worse, the rules ought to be changed.

What does this approach mean in regard to some of the controversial issues that confront us today? What about laws making divorce very difficult for all people regardless of their own religious beliefs? There are countries where legal divorce is impossible. Does this result in better marriages and better human beings, or does it produce "Divorce Italian Style"? Is murdering one's husband or wife in order to dissolve an impossible marriage really a better solution than a legal divorce? In fact, is it justifiable to force the religious convictions of people who reject divorce on other people who may not share the same religious beliefs? Do we not actually force one group's religious convictions on all groups when behavior considered immoral by one group is made illegal for all?

Or let us take another example: What about the laws against homosexuality? In most states sexual relations between consenting adults of the same sex are illegal and make the participants subject to severe penalties. Does this kind of law make people better, or does it merely encourage blackmail or even murder? Would it not be more constructive to have laws which encourage responsible human behavior without placing the pathological person at the mercy of the underworld, as our present laws often do? If homosexuality is a form of mental illness (as some experts believe), it is not very helpful to punish such people without trying to cure them.

We live in an age and in a country where the sexual instinct of human beings is being aggressively and commercially exploited to sell everything from automobiles to zithers. You are told that if you will only buy a certain toothpaste your mouth will have sex appeal. If only you use a certain grooming aid you will be pursued by beautiful women. Young and old are constantly assured that sex appeal is the most important achievement in life. But when people act on the basis of these exhortations, they are often rejected or even punished. Small wonder that we are raising a generation of mixed-up people who are constantly subjected to the double-bind, the contradictory exhortation to be seductive and virginal, aggressive and restrained. We know that one can drive rats insane in a laboratory by subjecting them constantly to contradictory stimuli, but we are doing it to an entire nation of which more than half are under 25 years of age—and we are surprised at the results of rape and riot.

While the Augsburg Confession does not deal with the subject of sexual morality in general, it does make concrete suggestions for the solution of the problems of sexual morality among the clergy. Since priests are human beings and most human beings need to express themselves sexually, priests should be allowed to marry. Marriage is the appropriate form of sexual expression for Christians. The reasonable and open way in which the Augsburg Confession confronts this controversial issue of its time could serve as a clue to the manner in which we should attack equally controversial issues in our time. What is needed is not prejudice and fanaticism but openness and reason. We should ask ourselves what kind of laws will help people live more human lives. What kind of laws will build a more harmonious and just human society? If the answers our study suggests mean that some laws have to be changed, so be it. Change of outmoded and unjust laws was the demand of Article XXIII of the Augsburg Confession. We cannot ask for less.

Article XXIV. The Mass

At the time of the Reformation the main religious service of the church was called "the Mass." It had received its name from the concluding Latin words of this service, and this name was retained by the adherents of the Reformation. Luther called his suggested reform of the service the "German Mass," and to this day the main service on Sunday in Swedish Lutheran churches is called "High Mass."

The controversy in the 16th century was not about whether the Mass should be abolished, but rather concerned its form and meaning. Thus the signers of the Augsburg Confession could say: "We are unjustly accused of having abolished the Mass. Without boasting, it is manifest that the Mass is observed among us with greater devotion and more earnestness than among our opponents. Moreover, the people are instructed often and with great diligence concerning the holy sacrament, why it was instituted, and how it is to be used (namely, as a comfort for terrified consciences) in order that the people may be drawn to the Communion and Mass" (Article XXIV).

The central argument was about the most adequate form for the Mass and its most faithful interpretation. The spokesmen for the Reformation advocated that the form of the Mass should make sense to the people and permit them to become involved in the worship of God. For this reason congregational singing was promoted, and Luther himself became a most successful hymnwriter. It also meant, of course, that the service had to be in the language of the people and not in some ancient ecclesiastical tongue which was no longer comprehensible to the worshipers. All these changes of form were made gradually, and the people were supposed to be instructed in order to be able to worship in a more meaningful manner.

The change in content was even more significant. The writers of the Augsburg Confession complained, "Before our time, the Mass came to be misused in many ways, . . . by turning it into a sort of fair, by buying and selling it, and by observing it in almost all churches for a monetary consideration." This sort of thing was abolished. Private Masses to be held for an individual gave way to the Mass as a service of the entire congregation. The Mass was no longer considered a "good work" or a sacrifice for sin but a service of worship for all the people in which the victory of Christ over evil and death was celebrated and in which the people were taught how they could celebrate this victory by living lives of service and love every day and in every walk of life.

The question which this article of the Augsburg Confession raises should also be asked in our time: Does the worship in our churches today meet the specification here set forth? Is the service understandable to people who join in it? Does it communicate the Christian Gospel, or does it obscure or even pervert it? To be faithful to the Augsburg Confession means today to remove the obstacles of form and content from all our worship. It is meaningless to argue from the situation of the 16th century, for many of the descendants of the opponents of the Augsburg Confession are today quite willing to try to reform their service. Are we as willing to make the necessary changes today as are our Roman Catholic brothers?

Let us first look at the form of our worship. Does the language of the typical Lutheran service make sense to the worshiping congregation? Do we really understand what we are saying, or are we merely going through the motions, so that it might as well be in

Latin? We may be asked to say in an introit: "He shall reward evil unto mine enemies: cut them off in thy truth" (Introit for the 26th Sunday after Trinity). Is this the kind of prayer with which we want to come before God at the beginning of our worship? It is English, even beautiful English, but does it make any kind of Christian sense? On Palm Sunday we pray in the introit that God should "deliver me from the horns of the unicorns." Are you positive that when you worship God on Palm Sunday this thought is uppermost in your mind? When were you last worried about being speared by a unicorn? I must admit it is very far down on my list of concerns. I am worried about cars and motorcycles and airplanes, but never about unicorns. Well, you may say, I know all that but I reinterpret those words so that they make sense to me. Well and good, but what about all those people who do not have your background and who think that one has to be at least half-crazy to use language like that?

Or look at the baptismal service. Most pastors ask the young parents who bring their child to be received into the people of God: "Do you renounce the devil, and all his works, and all his ways?" Remember, they do not have to ask this foolish question since it says in small print *"Then may the minister say,"* but most of them ask it anyway. What do you say? You do not even know what the question means. The word "renounce" means, according to my *Webster's Collegiate Dictionary*: "To give up, abandon, or resign." Who today does the opposite—"assert, maintain, and espouse" the devil? What good does it do to say words that cannot possibly mean anything to those who use them?

It seems obvious that if we are going to take the Augsburg Confession seriously, we will have to translate our service into the language of the man of today. That is what the Reformation did. To retain the formal language of the Reformation means to be unfaithful to its intent; we are true children of the Reformation only if we dare to be as contemporary in our language for our time as Luther was for his.

But more important than the form of the service is its content. The Augsburg Confession claimed that the purpose of the service is "to awaken our faith and comfort our consciences." This means that the Gospel has to be proclaimed so that people can understand it. But modern people are not used to instruction without discussion or illustration. We have to find new ways to reach them with the message of the Gospel, and we may have to learn from the experts of television and advertising. Dull speeches may have been a way of proclaiming the Gospel when people were used to listening to dull speeches, but this is no longer true; when somebody makes a dull speech on TV we change channels. In order to make worship meaningful today we have to find ways that fit our time. This is not the task of the pastor only; everybody has to be concerned and help. Especially young people—whose ears are attuned to the idiom of the day—can help the church to speak understandably.

If we do not understand our worship, it is senseless to be silent. Perhaps our churches need different types of services for different kinds of people. Those that worry about unicorns should have their day—but those who worry about war, air pollution, and rats should be heard too. The signers of the Augsburg Confession were laymen. If worship is to come alive in our time, we need equally concerned laymen today.

Article XXVII. Monastic Vows

Much of the work of the church in Luther's time was carried out by monks. Luther himself was an Augustinian monk, and most of his enemies were monks as well. The Reformation began in a monastery, and for a long time a monastery was its headquarters. Why, then, was Luther so opposed to monasticism, and why did the Augsburg Confession take such a completely negative stand on this issue?

The concluding words of Article XXVII are very clear: "There are many godless opinions associated with monastic vows: that they justify and render men righteous before God, that they constitute Christian perfection, that they are the means of fulfilling both evangelical counsels and precepts, and that they furnish the works of supererogation which we are not obligated to render to God."

There is not a word in this critique against all the useful contributions to the life of the church and to human civilization which the monks had actually made. For centuries monks had educated most of the Christian world. They had been eloquent preachers and leaders in works of Christian charity. Most of us will always remember the monks of St. Bernard who with the help of their dogs, the famous St. Bernards, rescued travelers who had lost their way in the snow and ice of the Alps.

Luther was not unfamiliar with the positive contributions which the monks had made. That he did not consider them inferior human beings is clearly demonstrated by the fact that many of his early associates in the work of reformation came from monasteries. One of the first martyrs to the cause of the Reformation was a Friar Henry of Zutphen (*A. E.* Vol. 32) who was lynched by a mob because of his effort to reform the church in northern Germany. It would be easy to show that without monks like Luther the Reformation would have been impossible. We must ask, then, Why this violent negative judgment in our Augsburg Confession?

The answer is "the godless opinions and errors associated with monastic vows." First of all, there was the claim some apparently made that a monk is a perfect human being, that his vow has made him righteous before God. This was hardly the official theology of the church of the time but it was an opinion held by many. Monastic vows were considered a dangerous form of self-deception by the signers of the Augsburg Confession. People would trust these vows rather than God's love—and this was bound to ruin them.

There was in fact much evidence that many monks had been lulled into a life of sloth and self-indulgence by their vows. The contemporary literature, written by good Catholics, frequently condemns monks as examples of irresponsibility, stupidity, and all kinds of actions subversive of the cause of Christ.

The second objection was that monastic vows made possible works of "supererogation." This complicated term means that, while God can rightly demand a limited kind of obedience from all men, monks do more than God demands. They accumulate a surplus of good works by their vows, and this surplus can be made available to those who are somewhat short—generally for a fee. The entire notion of a treasure of merits controlled by the church which she could dispense by means of indulgences was the actual occasion for the start of the Reformation. Thus, the notion of works of supererogation, works that are more than God demands of man, was offensive to the adherents of the Reformation.

Now, where does all this leave us today? First of all, we should probably go easy in our criticism of monasticism. The idea of people serving Christ in a disciplined way and as a disciplined community is certainly very useful. In some of the work of the church in difficult places here and abroad it is most likely the only way to accomplish anything. It does not have to be called monasticism, but the idea of a disciplined community serving God by serving men is as sound today as it was when the first monastic orders were organized.

Secondly, any claim that we can stand before God insisting on our own achievements is as unsound today as it was when the Augsburg Confession was written. Today among Protestants this claim is made in a somewhat different manner. We claim, often misquoting the martyred German theologian Dietrich Bonhoeffer, that we are people who have "come of age," that we are so much more mature than our parents or grandparents were before us, that God will have to deal with us on the basis of our achievements. We want recognition, not grace. We believe that with the help of our technology it will not be difficult to solve all of man's problems, that we are on the way to perfection—if not by way of monasticism then by way of education and the application of science to human society. The Augsburg Confession rejects all these pretensions. They may come today from entirely different people than the monks against whom our article thunders. We must recognize that these claims—to be independent of God and to have exceeded God's demands—are dangerous regardless of who makes them.

Thirdly, the idea that man can do more than God really wants him to do, that there are works of "supererogation," is as foolish today as it was in Luther's time. It assumes that there are certain works which we do for other men and still others which we do for ourselves. Man is divided like an apple: one segment belongs to God, another to the neighbors, and a third he keeps for himself. Then the argument begins: who should really get the largest part of the apple, and what is God's "proper" share?

The Augsburg Confession begins with the assumption that every man belongs entirely to God. All human life is properly service to God. What man does in his daily life is as much service to God as what he does for his family and for his church. All of life must be in line with the love which man knows he has received from God, and everything he does should be a response to it. Monastic vows are wrong because they suggest that there are only a few Christians who should live their lives in the presence of God, namely monks and nuns. In contrast, all who know that they are justified by grace also know that their entire life is an opportunity to express their gratitude to God for this love. As long as time lasts it will not be done perfectly, but it can at least be done gladly and out of a grateful heart.

Article XXVIII. The Power of Bishops

The final article of the Augsburg Confession (Article XXVIII) deals with the power of bishops. Two questions in particular are discussed: The relation of the leaders of the church to the temporal authorities, in short, the problem of church and state; and secondly, the right of the leaders of the church to regulate the life of the church itself.

On the first question the signers of the Augsburg Confession claimed that "the two authorities, the spiritual and the temporal, are not to be mingled or confused, for the spiritual power has its commission to preach the Gospel and administer the sacraments. Hence it should not invade the function of the other, should not set up and depose kings, should not annul temporal laws or undermine obedience to government, should not make or prescribe to the temporal power laws concerning worldly matters. . . . Thus our teachers distinguish the two authorities and the functions of the two powers, directing that both be held in honor as the highest gifts of God on earth."

The relevancy of this article to the present predicament of the church is striking. Does not this statement of the Augsburg Confession clearly tell all clergymen to keep out of politics? In a time when almost every day some minister, priest, or rabbi is arrested for leading a political parade protesting some domestic or foreign policy it seems as if the Augsburg Confession clearly stated that such participation on the part of the clergy is entirely wrong. The church, it says, should stay out of politics.

Before we accept this conclusion, however, we should remember the context in which this statement was made. In the 16th century many of the political rulers were at the same time bishops. The Augsburg Confession was protesting a situation which in American terms would mean that an appointment as president of a synod of the church in a state would also mean automatic appointment as governor of the same state. Such a situation seemed intolerable. We should also remember, however, that the Protestants (and particularly the Lutherans) did not improve matters by actually reversing the process and creating a situation where (speaking again in American terms) being the governor of a state also made you simultaneously the head of the church of that region.

The principle enunciated by the Augsburg Confession is that church and state have different basic objectives, so that confusing of the two institutions works out disastrously for both. This does not mean, however, that Christians can avoid participating in the life of both institutions. They must be members of the people of God as organized in the church and also of their nation as organized in the state. Membership in the church does not free you from your responsibilities for the nation; in fact it may make you actually more aware of these responsibilities. Similarly, being a law-abiding and tax-paying citizen does not relieve you of your responsibility for the work of the church, especially the proclamation of the Gospel.

In the light of the Augsburg Confession the clergyman has a responsibility to participate in political life like any other citizen. Being a minister does not give him special rights, nor does it give him the privilege to duck controversial issues because he lives allegedly in higher spheres.

If, therefore, a clergyman feels conscience-bound to march in a parade, he had better obey his conscience and go. As Luther said at the Diet of Worms, "It is not safe to go against conscience." This, however, does not mean that a clergyman has the right to bind the consciences of other people, even the members of his congregation, on these issues. If, for example, he claims that because *his* conscience tells *him* to protest the American involvement in war all the members of his congregation must take the same stand, he is wrong (as far as the Augsburg Confession is concerned) regardless of the merits of the American cause in the particular conflict.

On the other hand, if members of a congregation claim that their pastor has no right to express his political convictions simply because he is a pastor, they are equally wrong. To forbid clergymen to participate in the political life of this nation is as indefensible as forbidding them to marry. As citizens they have the right to responsible political action, and as Christians they have the duty. As human beings they have to take the chance that their most carefully made decisions may be wrong. We who do not believe in the infallibility of a pope certainly do not believe in the infallibility of a pastor either—whether we happen to agree with him on a particular issue or not. The Augsburg Confession denies the right of the church to prescribe to the temporal power laws concerning worldly matters, but it does not stop any citizen, be he clergyman or layman, from participating in the political life of his country according to the dictates of his conscience.

This article also has a second thrust. It defines the authority of pastors and bishops as follows: "Bishops or pastors may make regulations so that everything in the churches is done in good order, but not as a means of obtaining God's grace or making satisfaction for sins, nor in order to bind men's consciences by considering these things necessary services of God and counting it a sin to omit their observance even when this is done without offense."

We live in an age of great and rapid changes in all aspects of our life. The Augsburg Confession tells us that we should not be afraid of change in the church either. But changes should be made with a purpose. The one question the church must always ask is: Does such a change help men to know Christ and his Gospel? It seems that many aspects of the church's life have little to do with the proclamation of the Gospel. Are we sure that we do not need certain changes today to allow the Gospel to break out of our churches and into the world?

Is the organization of the church adequate to the needs of our time? One of the worst features of the organized church is its inability to handle criticism and to correct mistakes. In the political realm we have an organized opposition which by its criticism keeps the people in power alert and if they are not alert removes them at the next election. In the church organized criticism is forbidden. The so-called "ecclesiastical ballot," which makes it impossible to elect men in relation to issues and makes every election in the church into a popularity contest, is an invention of the devil. Nobody is allowed to say why he supports person "A" against person "B" for a certain office. Perhaps such an approach made some sense when synods and denominations were small and everybody knew everybody else, but today this approach is destructive of the intent of the democratic process. Change in the organization of the church is desperately needed to make it a more adequate instrument of the Gospel for the final decades of the 20th century and to prepare for the 21st. The Augsburg Confession not only allows for change but actually encourages it. The question is: Are we willing to meet the challenge?

Conclusion

In the preceding chapters we looked at the Augsburg Confession with the eyes of people living in the final decades of the 20th century, and we became aware of the fact that our cultural situation is entirely different from that of the 16th century. Indeed, our environment is so unlike that of 16th century Germany that some of the problems faced by the Augsburg Confession seem quite unreal to us.

As we look back, therefore, we want to ask again—is there anything really significant for our time in this venerable document of the faith of the church? What can we learn for the present from our brief study of the Augsburg Confession?

First of all, the Augsburg Confession tells us who we are by telling us where we came from. A very important part of having a religious commitment is its involvement with the past. A person who is religiously committed accepts, among other things, a historical-cultural tradition. This is not all that religious commitment implies, but it is a significant part of it. Religious commitment means for most of us identifying with a particular tradition and accepting it as our own. This religious tradition may be Hindu or Buddhist; it may be Zuni or Dobu; it may also be Jewish or Christian. The Augsburg Confession helps us to understand the historical dimension of this commitment.

To take the Augsburg Confession seriously is a form of self-acceptance. It is the admission that this is the kind of man I am. These are my antecedents, this is my history, this is how I came to be who I am. In a sense it is a commitment to history. It does not have to be dishonest or uncritical, but it is important for me in order that I may know who I am. The study of the Augsburg Confession should have made it easier for the reader who shares its tradition to understand who he is because it has indicated where he came from. For the reader who does not share this tradition, it should have made it easier to understand his neighbors because he has gained some insight into their background.

Secondly, the Augsburg Confession tells us that men must take a stand. Thought must eventuate into action. Theological positions which involve not the entire community of faith but only its leadership are in the long run not very important. While the Augsburg Confession was written by a professor of theology, it was signed by all kinds of laymen who had never studied theology. It was important because it involved these laymen. Most of the statements of the churches in our time are so trivial because everybody knows that they involve only a committee, and not even the membership of this committee very deeply. The people who signed the Augsburg Confession knew that signing might cost them their jobs, perhaps even their lives. They felt it was worth it.

As long as theological statements are only words that do not obligate us in any way they are not worth the paper they are written on. The critics of the Christian church are convinced that there is nothing behind all this Christian rhetoric. They believe that Christians use words as a substitute for action, talking about life and love, compassion and forgiveness so that they do not have to live and love, suffer and forgive. It is significant that the Augsburg Confession committed the entire community of faith confessing it to action. It was not a substitute for action but a symbol of the action in which all these men and women were actually involved every day.

Thirdly, the Augsburg Confession calls us to remember that we

all live "After the Fall." One of the favorite pastimes of religious
people seems to be to distinguish between those who are "good"
and those who are "bad," according to their particular standards
of evaluation. These groups may be labeled "believers" and "infidels,"
"righteous" and "sinners," the "saved" and the "lost," those who are
"with it" and those who are not. There are innumerable labels, all
tending to obscure the fact that all men are living "After the Fall"
as infidels, sinners, and lost who are indeed "out of it." It is this fact
of our estrangement from God, from each other, and from ourselves
that we all have in common. It is the realization of this universal
human condition which makes the brotherhood of man possible
and imperative. Because we are all without exception in this pre-
carious situation, all the differences of class and caste, intelligence
and beauty, or wealth and power are utterly insignificant. All men
have far more in common than can possibly separate them.

To feel superior to any other man reveals abysmal ignorance of
the nature of the human predicament. The Augsburg Confession
can help us today to recognize the seriousness of the human situation against all the naive, ill-informed, and sentimental optimism
which blinds us to the facts and thus makes any solution impossible.
Since so many of the peddlers of such optimism claim to be Christian theologians, the realism of the Augsburg Confession is of
special significance in our time.

Fourthly, the Augsburg Confession tells us that Christianity, the
church, and the organizations of the church have only one purpose
—namely to confront men and women with Christ. There are
many other important tasks, but these are done better by other
organizations and agencies. But if the Christian church fails to
confront men with Christ, this confrontation will not take place.
It is possible to use an automobile as a clothes closet or to raise
mushrooms in the trunk of a car, but a car is primarily a means of
transportation; you cannot go to work in a clothes closet or drive
to the seashore in a mushroom bed. The Augsburg Confession reminds us that unless the Christian church proclaims Christ it is a

second rate imitation of a political party, a school, a social club, or a sensitivity training meeting. The criterion for the validity of all claims of the church to be God's people is its eloquence in word and deed about Jesus as the Christ. If it is mute at this point, it is a cheap imitation of something else and travels under false colors.

Fifthly, law is an aid to man and supports his freedom; it does not destroy it. Today as in the 16th century many people seem to see freedom and law as opposite to each other, but the Augsburg Confession considers law the condition of freedom. This is true in every area of life. It is the "due process of law" which protects our life against chaos and brutality. It is because of traffic laws that we are able to drive more or less safely across the country and that airplanes can move millions of people across the face of this earth. Without such law, all freedom of movement would in fact disappear. To let any airplane fly at will without regard to the control tower makes all airplane travel hazardous and eventually impossible. It is the law which protects minorities against the tyranny of the majorities. It allows Jehovah's Witnesses to hold services in the city park and keeps the majority from telling you what books you may read or may not read.

Lawlessness and anarchy are not the road to freedom but to tyranny. Because the signers of the Augsburg Confession knew that, they opposed lawlessness and saw in it the poison which would destroy their freedom and the freedom of all other men. In our age, where lawlessness seems to some the shortest road to freedom, the Augsburg Confession expresses a warning which we will ignore only at our own great peril. "Due process of law" in the family, in the church, in village and city, in the nation, and in the relationship among the nations is the only hope for lasting freedom for all men. The alternative to law is the rule of the gunslinger, whether he carries a .45 or a hydrogen bomb.

And finally, the Augsburg Confession assures us that the problem of man is man. Any analysis of the human situation which ignores this basic truth is bound to do more damage than good. We have the power to make man live longer, but longer does not necessarily mean better. Some men, we can all recall, lived entirely too long, and mankind has suffered because of it.

We are able and willing to change the world drastically in every conceivable way, but to change does not necessarily mean to improve. Many of the changes we have the power to bring about would tend to abolish man and turn him into a robot or a monster. We *can* do many things now which we probably *should not* do. It is a tragic fallacy to assume that we should do everything we have the power to do. But to avoid the disastrous identification of "can do" and "should do," we must always remember that the problem of man is man and only a better man can safeguard a better world.

The Augsburg Confession is not afraid of value judgments, and unless we are willing to make value judgments the time will come very soon when we will no longer have the opportunity to choose. To be neutral between good and evil is not wholesome objectivity but suicidal foolishness. The Augsburg Confession is a document of partisanship, not of neutrality. It advocates partisanship for Christ and the Gospel and tries to enlist all readers in this cause.

We live in an age of great decisions. Nothing is sacrosanct. Nothing will be kept merely because it is old and traditional. The Augsburg Confession can help us in our time because it suggests helpful criteria for the changes which we will have to make. Change is necessary and unavoidable. Christians who are pilgrims on the way into God's future are not afraid of change. To be a pilgrim means to live constantly in the presence of change. But a pilgrim also wants to reach a goal. Running around in circles is not a pilgrimage. The Augsburg Confession may help us find our bearings for our pilgrimage toward tomorrow.